# Promoting and Delivering School-to-School Support for Special Educational Needs

Recent changes to education policy have brought about a new emphasis on promoting school-to-school support and school-led improvement in order to ensure that all pupils, including those with special educational needs (SEN), achieve their optimum potential. Special educational needs coordinators (SENCOs), often in the role of specialist leaders of education, now undertake coaching, mentoring and the delivery of training to ensure that trainee, newly qualified and experienced teachers and teaching assistants have the practical skills to effectively meet the needs of pupils with SEN.

In her trademark down-to-earth style, Rita Cheminais shows SENCOs how to respond to and enhance this exciting and pivotal new role by:

- explaining the new school-to-school support and school-led improvement context that many SENCOs will be working in;
- clarifying the role of the outstanding SENCO, as a specialist leader of education;
- maximising the best practice arising from the effective use of the pupil premium and the Achievement for All initiative;
- confirming OFSTED's expectations for special educational needs and disability in the revised inspection schedule for schools and academies;
- describing how best to monitor, evaluate and validate best practice in school-to-school support.

Packed with time-saving photocopiable resources, examples of best practice and further activities for reflection, this practical book will enable the SENCO to respond to the current agenda, particularly in performing the role of a specialist leader of education, disseminating SEN expertise across schools.

*Promoting and Delivering School-to-School Support for Special Educational Needs* is essential reading for all outstanding and aspiring-outstanding SENCOs working in the early years, primary, secondary and special phases of education, academies and Pupil Referral Units.

**Rita Cheminais** is a freelance education consultant, author and national speaker.

**nasen** is a professional membership association that supports all those who work with or care for children and young people with special and additional educational needs. Members include teachers, teaching assistants, support workers, other educationalists, students and parents.

**nasen** supports its members through policy documents, journals, its magazine *Special!*, publications, professional development courses, regional networks and newsletters. Its website contains more current information such as responses to government consultations. **nasen's** published documents are held in very high regard both in the UK and internationally.

Other titles published in association with the National Association for Special Educational Needs (**nasen**):

**Brilliant Ideas for Using ICT in the Inclusive Classroom**
*Sally McKeown and Angela McGlashon*

**Language for Learning in the Secondary School**
A practical guide for supporting students with speech, language and communication needs
*Sue Hayden and Emma Jordan*

**ADHD: All Your Questions Answered**
A complete handbook for SENCOs and teachers
*Fintan O'Regan*

**Assessing Children with Specific Learning Difficulties**
A teacher's practical guide
*Gavin Reid, Gad Elbeheri and John Everatt*

**Using Playful Practice to Communicate with Special Children**
*Margaret Corke*

**The Equality Act for Educational Professionals**
A simple guide to disability and inclusion in schools
*Geraldine Hills*

**More Trouble with Maths**
A teacher's complete guide to identifying and diagnosing mathematical difficulties
*Steve Chinn*

**Dyslexia and Inclusion**
Classroom approaches for assessment, teaching and learning, 2nd edition
*Gavin Reid*

**Promoting and Delivering School-to-School Support for Special Educational Needs**
A practical guide for SENCOs
*Rita Cheminais*

# Promoting and Delivering School-to-School Support for Special Educational Needs

A practical guide for SENCOs

Rita Cheminais

Routledge
Taylor & Francis Group

LONDON AND NEW YORK

nasen
Helping Everyone Achieve

First published 2013
by Routledge
2 Park Square, Milton Park, Abingdon, Oxon OX14 4RN

Simultaneously published in the USA and Canada
by Routledge
711 Third Avenue, New York, NY 10017

*Routledge is an imprint of the Taylor & Francis Group, an informa business*

*British Library Cataloguing in Publication Data*
A catalogue record for this book is available from the British Library

*Library of Congress Cataloging in Publication Data*
A catalog record for this book has been requested

ISBN: 978-0-415-63370-3 (pbk)
ISBN: 978-0-203-09489-1 (ebk)

Typeset in Galliard
by GreenGate Publishing Services, Tonbridge, Kent

eResources for this title are available at **www.routledge.com/9780415633703.**

Printed and bound in Great Britain by MPG Printgroup

# Contents

# List of figures and tables

# Acknowledgements

I would like to thank all the SENCOs that I have had the privilege to work with over the past twelve months, for their feedback in identifying the key training and continuing professional development they feel they need, in order to meet the coalition government's education agenda.

I would also like to thank the headteachers in Tameside, who have supported me in developing ideas for this book, particularly in relation to school-to-school support.

Most importantly, I would like to thank Alison Foyle and Rhiannon Findlay, from Routledge Education, for guiding and supporting me throughout the production of this book.

I wish to thank the Sutton Trust Education Endowment Foundation for granting permission to include the pupil premium approaches and their effectiveness represented in Table 4.2, the Teaching Leaders organisation for their permission to make reference to the five stages of the teaching leader learning journey, in Table 1.3, and the National College for School Leadership for giving their permission to feature some of the areas of expertise from the *Specialist Leaders of Education Prospectus*, listed in Table 2.1.

# List of abbreviations

| | |
|---|---|
| **ACAS** | Advisory, Conciliation and Arbitration Service |
| **AEN** | additional educational needs |
| **AfA** | Achievement for All |
| **AfL** | Assessment for Learning |
| **APP** | assessing pupil progress |
| **ASD** | autistic spectrum disorder |
| **AST** | advanced skills teacher |
| **BESD** | behavioural, emotional and social difficulties |
| **CPD** | continuing professional development |
| **DCSF** | Department for Children, Schools and Families |
| **DfE** | Department for Education |
| **EAL** | English as an additional language |
| **EHCP** | education, health and care plan |
| **FSM** | free school meals |
| **GCSE** | General Certificate of Secondary Education |
| **GROW** | goals, reality, options, will |
| **HE** | Higher Education |
| **HLTA** | higher level teaching assistant |
| **HMI** | Her Majesty's Inspector |
| **ICT** | information and communication technology |
| **IEP** | individual education plan |
| **INSET** | in-service education and training |
| **ITP** | improving teacher programme |
| **ITT** | initial teacher training |
| **KS** | Key Stage |
| **LA** | local authority |
| **LAC** | looked after child |
| **LLE** | local leader of education |
| **MFL** | modern foreign language |
| **MLD** | moderate learning difficulties |
| **NCSL** | National College for School Leadership |
| **NLE** | national leader of education |
| **NQT** | newly qualified teacher |
| **NSS** | national support school |
| **NUT** | National Union of Teachers |

| | |
|---|---|
| **OFSTED** | Office for Standards in Education, Children's Services and Skills |
| **OTP** | outstanding teacher programme |
| **PASS** | pupil attitude to self and school |
| **PE** | physical education |
| **PRU** | Pupil Referral Unit |
| **QA** | quality assurance |
| **QFT** | quality first teaching |
| **SEN** | special educational needs |
| **SENCO** | special educational needs coordinator |
| **SEND** | special educational needs and disability |
| **SISS** | self-improving school system |
| **SLD** | severe learning difficulties |
| **SLE** | specialist leader of education |
| **SLT** | senior leadership team |
| **TA** | teaching assistant |
| **TDA** | Training and Development Agency for Schools |
| **VA** | value added |
| **VLE** | virtual learning environment |

# Introduction

## The aim of this book

Whether you are a newly appointed SENCO promoting and developing school-to-school support for SEND, or an experienced SENCO leading school-to-school support for SEND, this book aims to:

- clarify what the new role for SENCOs entails in the 21st century;
- identify the essential skills and knowledge required by SENCOs to promote and lead change in SEND;
- explore the concept and principles of school-to-school support for SEND;
- examine the good practice of Achievement for All and show how SENCOs can implement this initiative, within and beyond their own school;
- determine what is the most effective use of the pupil premium and how SENCOs can disseminate what works well at local SENCO networks;
- clarify the Office for Standards in Education, Children's Services and Skills (OFSTED) school inspection expectations in relation to SEND;
- provide guidance on how best to quality assure school-to-school support for SEND.

## Educational developments influencing new role for SENCOs

The educational landscape at the time of writing this book has changed rapidly under the leadership of the coalition government. Michael Gove, the Secretary of State for Education, on 28th July 2010, at an Education Select Committee meeting commented: 'The haste is because I believe that we desperately need to transform our educational system'.

Competition has reappeared in the educational marketplace, resulting in outstanding schools being encouraged by the government to convert to academy status. Free schools have also been established, although not necessarily in areas of social deprivation, as first intended by the coalition government.

Academies and free schools are independent from local authority (LA) control. With the 'culling' of the local authority children's services, and the establishment of teaching schools, the move towards school-to-school improvement support in the maintained education sector has progressed very quickly. This development has helped to further strengthen the existing collaborative partnership working between schools, via clusters, federations and learning networks.

Local authority school improvement advisers and officers are things of the past. Outstanding headteachers, working as national leaders of education, and local leaders of education, are taking on the school improvement role of the LA.

Similarly, outstanding school senior and middle leaders, in the role of a specialist leader of education (SLE), and outstanding middle leaders in the role of a teaching leader, both of which are applicable to outstanding SENCOs, are also helping to improve standards in the quality of teaching, and the competence of teachers, through coaching and mentoring, and demonstrating outstanding practice.

Schools also have greater control over their school budgets, which includes how they utilise the additional pupil premium funding for their most disadvantaged pupils. SENCOs are likely to be engaged in aspects of how the pupil premium has been utilised, as several children on free school meals (FSM) and looked after children (LAC) may also be likely to have SEND.

The coalition government's heightened focus on improving the quality of teaching is reflected in the current OFSTED school and academy inspection framework, introduced in January 2012.

The Department for Education (DfE), in their White Paper entitled *The Importance of Teaching*, commented:

> We will consider how to support the identification of excellence in teaching for pupils with special educational needs (whether in special or mainstream schools) so that the strongest practice can be shared, including through Teaching Schools.
>
> (DfE 2010b: 7.9)

Christine Blower, General Secretary of the National Union of Teachers (NUT), voiced concerns over the break-up of the existing school system, and the implications of this on the role of the SENCO, in her contribution to the Labour Party's *Special Educational Needs Policy Review* in March 2012. She commented:

> The massive pressure is on SENCOs to work beyond their skill sets, when they are already overworked, carrying out several other roles within the school.

It is interesting that the Labour Party felt the need for this review of SEN policy, despite the coalition government's *Next Steps* recommendations. However, it is encouraging to know that the shadow government is still taking an interest in SEND.

The role of the SENCO is going to change dramatically over the next five years, irrespective of which political party is in office. The 2008 SENCO regulations are already in need of an urgent revision, in light of the coalition government's evolutionary changes to the SEND system, including school-to-school support.

## How the book is designed to be used

The book can be worked through systematically in chapter order, or it can be dipped into, focusing on particular areas of interest. Either way, this practical book provides an invaluable resource that can be used to:

- act as a quick point of reference for busy senior leaders and SENCOs working in schools and academies, as well as for those leading teaching schools, who are brokering and commissioning SENCOs as SLEs;
- help inform the nature of school-to-school support for SEND, in response to the latest coalition government legislation and changes in SEND;
- provide photocopiable and downloadable resources for developmental purposes within and beyond the educational setting, across a teaching school alliance or in a SENCO network.

The layout of each chapter provides:

- an initial summary of the key content of the chapter;
- the latest up-to-date information on the chapter theme and focus;
- checklists offering practical guidance and top tips;
- cameos of good practice;
- photocopiable and downloadable resources, many of which can be customised and tailored to suit the context of the individual educational setting, or the teaching school alliance;
- useful points to remember;
- further activities for reflection.

# Chapter 1

# Opportunities and challenges for SENCOs

---

**This chapter covers:**

- Opportunities for SENCOs in the 21st century and implications for their role
- Challenges for SENCOs in an era of educational change
- A new role for SENCOs
- Essential knowledge and skills to support the SENCO's new role
- The origin, concept and development of the teaching school

---

## Opportunities for SENCOs in the 21st century and implications for their role

The coalition government has overhauled the outdated thirty-three-year-old special educational needs system, and modernised the SEN Code of Practice. This has resulted in SENCOs having a far more manageable workload, in relation to having fewer children identified with SEN, on the new single early years setting and school-based category of SEN. In turn, SENCOs have gained some more time to focus on their strategic role leading, innovating, monitoring and evaluating SEN, across the educational setting.

The disappearance of individual education plans (IEPs), replaced with a single education, health and care plan for pupils previously statemented with SEN that exceed what is normally available in the early years setting, the school, academy or college, has resulted in the streamlining of the SEN paperwork, with responsibilities for SEN provision being more fairly distributed, across external agencies and voluntary, community organisations, making the assessment and review process less bureaucratic and stressful for SENCOs, parents and SEN pupils. The DfE in their SEND Green Paper (2011), stated:

> We need to reduce the burdens that are currently placed on our schools, particularly on SENCOs.
>
> (DfE 2011c: 5.2)

The downsizing and simplification of the educational settings SEN policy, making it more parent- and family-friendly, provides an excellent opportunity for SENCOs to revisit this document and consult with a range of key stakeholders, i.e. governors, staff, parents, pupils and external partners, in order to clarify the new changes in the SEN system.

SENCOs, looking for a new direction in their leadership and teaching career, now have a wider range of educational settings to work in, e.g. academies and free schools, both independent from local authority control.

The revised OFSTED school and academy inspection framework, introduced in September 2012, places greater emphasis on SEN and disability (SEND), offering SENCOs a further opportunity to build capacity among staff for SEND, within and beyond their own educational setting, to share experiences of inspection and disseminate best practice via SENCO networks or teaching school alliances.

The introduction of teaching schools, with their alliance of partner schools and other members, such as a university, LA or independent consultant, offers outstanding SENCOs, with at least three or more years senior or middle leadership experience in the role, the chance to become an SLE, and use their SEN expertise to support another school, requiring significant improvement in this aspect.

## Challenges for SENCOs in an era of educational change

SENCOs will have the initial challenge of securing a quality input on the new SEN changes in the educational setting's annual in-service education and training (INSET) programme. This will be vital to ensure governors, senior and middle leaders, teachers, support staff, including administrative staff, are familiar with the new SEN system and changes. In addition, the SENCO will need to request some additional non-contact time in order to revise their SEN register, SEN policy and internal SEN system and paperwork. Figure 1.1 offers a model SEN policy reflecting the new SEN system.

Balancing the wider school-to-school support role with work in their own school poses a challenge for SENCOs, particularly in relation to not compromising or depressing SEN standards in their own educational setting because they have been out supporting another school. Some outstanding SENCOs prefer to become a teaching leader, where they work with a new SEN department in their own school to build capacity among their SEN team. The revised SEN Code of Practice and the new SEN legislation brought in by the coalition government, effective by 2014, are likely to result in SENCOs reviewing the role and effective deployment of teaching assistants, and other supporting adults, in a streamlined SEN system within a 21st-century context.

SENCOs are going to be challenged to broker and commission services and support from local services and voluntary, community organisations, as parents of SEN pupils begin to have their own budgets for SEN. As LA services for SEND downsize and/or disappear with the government cuts to LA spending, SENCOs are going to have to become far more creative in managing diminishing SEN resources. SENCOs, like headteachers, are going to have to explore funding and sharing additional services for SEN across a cluster or federation of schools. Academy status does offer a greater opportunity to purchase their own external professionals for SEN, as they are independent from the LA.

Outstanding SENCOs, who become SLEs, will face the added challenge of undertaking further professional development to enhance their skills and knowledge of how to undertake school-to-school support for SEN, with maximum effectiveness.

Table 1.1 provides a force field analysis template for SENCOs to use in identifying the opportunities and challenges they are likely to meet, which could be completed with their line manager.

SENCOs may find Figure 1.2, the SENCO checklist for preparing to introduce the new SEN changes to a range of different stakeholders in their own educational setting, useful. This can be tailored and adapted to suit the context of the educational setting.

## WELCOME TO MAPLE SCHOOL

### SEN POLICY

### A LEAFLET FOR PARENTS

*The education, health and care plan (EHCP)*

The EHCP sets out the pupil's SEN; the expected outcomes for the child; the SEN provision required, as well as any health and social care provision.

The EHCP will also name the preferred school or academy, after the governing body and the headteacher have confirmed they can meet the child's SEN. The EHCP is reviewed annually.

*What SEN provision is in school?*

The extra or different SEN provision may include: support from a specialist teacher; access to a specialist teaching programme; specialist ICT equipment and/or software; or it may be health care provision such as physiotherapy, or speech and language therapy; or it may be one-to-one counselling and/or pastoral and academic mentoring.

*Who is the SEN coordinator?*

Mr. Mike Irvine is the SENCO and the SEN governor is Mrs. Potts.

This leaflet gives a summary of Maple School's new SEN policy, which has been updated to meet the latest government changes in SEN.

Parents of SEN pupils in the school have worked together to produce this leaflet in parent-friendly language. The leaflet can be viewed on and downloaded from the school's website at: www.mapleschool.sch.uk/sen.

If you require a copy of this leaflet in different languages and formats, then do call in at the school office, to pick one up in the version you prefer.

The school's SEN policy is reviewed annually, and revised as and when SEN law changes.

*What is the 'local offer'?*

The local authority publishes its 'local offer', i.e. the provision and services available for children with SEN. This local offer includes information about:

– how to get an EHC needs assessment;
– other sources of information, advice and support for children with SEN and their parents/carers who look after them;
– getting access to extra and different provision, including training and travel to and from school, college or university;
– how to make a complaint about provision.

The 'local offer' of the local authority is kept under review. The 'local offer' can be found on the local authority website: www.anyla@sen.gov.uk or at the local council offices on the ground floor, at reception.

*Which pupils have SEN?*

A pupil has SEN if they have difficulty learning or a disability which needs extra or different provision (SEN provision) from that which is provided for other children of the same age in their mainstream class. A SEN pupil will have had a single *Education, Health and Care Needs Assessment* to confirm their special educational needs.

Some children with the most complex and severe learning difficulties and/or disability will have an EHCP put in place, following the single EHCP needs assessment.

Other children with SEN who have less complex needs will not have an EHCP because they will manage to access learning in the classroom with the help of high-quality teaching, curriculum differentiation, in-class support from a teaching assistant and pastoral care.

*Outcomes for SEN pupils at school*

All SEN pupils are expected to achieve their personal best, through the extra and different provision they receive. Their attainment and progress is tracked and monitored each term, year on year. SEN pupil progress is judged from their starting point on entry to school, and also year on year, at the end of each academic year, across the curriculum. Pupils who receive extra literacy support are expected to make twice the amount of progress from when they started the programme.

*Personal budgets for SEN*

Parents will be supported and advised by the SENCO in school as to how best to spend their personal budget for SEN for their child.

*Complaints procedure for SEN*

Parents should refer to the school's complaints policy and procedure.

*Figure 1.1* Model leaflet for parents summarising the school's new SEN policy

*Table 1.1* Force field analysis – opportunities and challenges to SENCO role

| FORCE FIELD ANALYSIS FOR SENCOs | |
| --- | --- |
| The priority for the SENCO in introducing the new SEN system into the school | |
| *FORCES PROMOTING POSITIVE CHANGE* | *FORCES OF CHALLENGE ACTING AS BARRIERS TO CHANGE* |
| *STRATEGIES FOR SUSTAINABLE IMPLEMENTATION OF THE NEW SEN SYSTEM* | |

☑ SENCO familiarises themselves with the new SEN changes and prepares a briefing paper for the senior leadership team (SLT).

☑ Meet the headteacher and SLT to discuss national SEN changes and agree extra non-contact time to establish new SEN system in school, and book a slot on school continuing professional development (CPD) programme on SEN.

☑ Meet with the SEN governor and discuss the new SEN changes and the implications for the SEN governor role. Agree a programme of termly meetings to monitor implementation of the new SEN system in school.

☑ Meet with middle leaders (subject coordinators, phase/key stage leaders and aspect coordinators, e.g. assessment coordinator) to inform them of the new SEN system and agree how they will monitor implementation in their subject/aspect/phase area.

☑ Meet with the SEN team, e.g. teaching assistants, learning mentors, to prepare them for the new SEN system and changes, and discuss the implications for their role and new ways of working.

☑ Deliver whole school INSET on SEN changes to staff, inviting governors.

☑ Revise SEN policy, downsizing this, and making it parent-friendly.

☑ Revise the SEN development plan, using distributed leadership, to share out activities among SEN team and senior leaders.

☑ Inform parents and pupils of the SEN changes and what the benefits will be for them.

☑ Begin to develop and customise new SEN proforma, to support the education, health and care plan process.

☑ Offer a drop-in session for staff, once a week, in the first term of implementation of the new SEN system, to answer any queries.

☑ SENCO to meet with the line manager to review how SEN changes are going, and to identify any further support to improve implementation.

☑ SENCO to attend local SENCO network to share best practice in relation to implementing new SEN systems, and bring back ideas for further improvement in SEN.

*Figure 1.2* SENCO checklist for preparing to introduce SEN changes

## A new role for SENCOs

The SENCO regulations of 2008 require further expansion, and savvy SENCOs are already facing up to the challenge to review their current job description, with their line manager and/or headteacher. The type of additional tasks to add to the current SENCO job description include:

- Informing decisions about the use of the pupil premium, and evaluating the impact of any pupil premium interventions they have been responsible for.
- Undertaking school-to-school support for SEN and evaluating the impact of this work.
- Managing some SEN funding across a cluster, federation or alliance of schools, to secure external services for SEN pupils.
- Supporting parents and families of SEN children in making best use of their personal SEN budgets.
- Overseeing the education, health and care plans of SEN pupils.
- Advising on the best form of portable information and communication technology (ICT) for SEN pupils to use within and beyond the school, especially to continue their learning outside school, where they may be off for a long time recovering from surgery, e.g. iPad, iPod, giving access to a virtual learning environment (VLE).
- Acting as an interim executive SENCO in a school requiring significant improvement in SEN, where a SENCO may have left or retired from an educational setting.

The SENCO's personal challenge will be to review their job description with their line manager/ headteacher, in light of these changes.

## Essential knowledge and skills to support the SENCO's new role

Table 1.2 identifies the knowledge and skills essential for SENCOs in an era of school-to-school support for SEN. The knowledge and skills are appropriate for newly appointed SENCOs, those with two or three years' experience or very experienced veteran SENCOs.

*Table 1.2* Essential knowledge and skills for SENCOs

| SENCO knowledge | SENCO skills |
| --- | --- |
| 1 Know the principles of school-to-school support, in relation to school improvement for SEN. | 1 Able to transfer SENCO expertise and leadership strategies when implementing SEN changes in another school context. |
| 2 Know about change management and the appropriate strategies for change, to use in implementing the new SEN system. | 2 Skills of diplomacy, using emotional intelligence to get the best out of staff who are anxious/unsure about change for SEN. |
| 3 Know the basics of resonant leadership and system-wide leadership, to take the wider view. | 3 Skills in managing conflict and effectively communicating with challenging stakeholders, i.e. parents, staff. |
| 4 Know the best ways in which to turn round a significantly underperforming school in the aspect of SEN. | 4 Skills of analysis to identify priorities in SEN, and make recommendations and offer solutions for improvement in SEN. |
| 5 Know the basics of effective human resource management, and distributed leadership, in deploying supporting adults for SEN. | 5 Skills of resilience, in order to cope with any set-backs, opposition to new roles or barriers to promoting new ways of working for SEN staff and teaching assistants (TAs). |
| 6 Know the new OFSTED inspection framework, with particular relevance to SEND. | 6 Skills in achieving consistency in SEN practice in own school and other educational settings. |
| 7 Know about coaching and mentoring at a deeper level of learning, in particular, how to apply the goals, reality, options, will (GROW) model of coaching. | 7 Skills of coaching and mentoring to use with other staff, to build their self-confidence, and modelling best practice in SEN. |
| 8 Know the four strands of Achievement for All, which aims to improve SEN pupils' outcomes. | 8 Skills in implementing new initiatives and ideas with confidence, being able to adapt a strategy for different schools and SEN contexts. |
| 9 Know which additional interventions and strategies work best, in relation to making best use of the pupil premium. | 9 Skills in making best use of resources, including additional funding, to achieve best value in relation to pupil outcomes. |
| 10 Know how to undertake small-scale, school-based action research and appreciative inquiry to explore an aspect of SEN which requires improvement. | 10 Skills in monitoring and evaluating SEN policy and provision, in order to show improvement and areas for further development. |
| 11 Know how best to collate, analyse and use SEN pupil-level data with staff, to inform improvement. | 11 Skills in interpreting different types of data (quantitative and qualitative), to validate outcomes. |
| 12 Know how to undertake SEN pupil-centred reviews. | 12 Skills in using a range of different communication methods, to strengthen and empower pupil voice. |
| 13 Know how to utilise the structured conversation with parents/families of SEN pupils. | 13 Skills in negotiation and facilitating parent partnership and parent/family voice. |

### Resonant leadership skills for SENCOs

SENCOs, as resonant leaders, are able to energise those around them, especially in times of change and uncertainty, i.e. implementing a revised SEN system.

There are five key characteristics of resonant leaders:

1  **Know themselves and are able to develop their own leadership skills**, i.e. the SENCO is authentic, genuine, self-aware and tunes in well to those they lead. They know their own strengths and weaknesses, and can tailor their leadership style to the context of their educational setting.

2  **Able to motivate and energise others**. The SENCO is confident to lead by example, and can relate to staff concerns about SEN. They are able to make staff see the bigger picture for SEN, and are present for staff when needed. The SENCO encourages staff to practise and try out new SEN approaches or initiatives, acknowledging the success of these staff.

3  **Focus on improvement in SEN**, i.e. particularly in relation to ensuring better outcomes for SEN pupils. The SENCO will challenge underperformance rigorously. The SENCO is realistic about expected outcomes from new initiatives for SEN. For example, they are aware that generally only one in five new initiatives are usually successful. The outward-facing and outward-looking SENCO seeks new ways of problem solving. The SENCO seeks evidence-based practice, as to what works best in relation to SEN. They are proactive in developing staff in order to improve the quality of SEN provision. For example, the SENCO may suggest to senior leaders in the school which teachers would be eligible for engaging in the outstanding teacher programme (OTP) or the improving teacher programme (ITP). They nurture, empower and encourage staff with the potential to risk take and try out new ways of working, in order to improve outcomes for SEN pupils.

4  **Collaborate with others and are collaborative themselves**, i.e. the SENCO knows that they cannot achieve improvement and change in SEN alone: Together Each Achieves More (TEAM). SENCOs develop a presence and credibility not only within their own educational setting, but also across a local SENCO cluster or alliance of schools. They know that by working collaboratively with others within and beyond their own educational setting, they will become more effective in solving problems and dealing with any challenges relating to SEN. The SENCO is savvy in choosing only those collaborations that will be the most beneficial in improving outcomes for SEN pupils. They are willing to share their own good practice with other SENCOs, as well as learning from outstanding SENCOs and school leaders.

5  **Able to develop a compelling narrative that others believe in**, i.e. resonant SENCO leaders are able to read the changing SEN context and help those they lead to understand and cope with the change. The SENCO is aspirational and positive in their vision and strategy, making the implementation of new SEN policy and practice appear achievable to staff. They are able to let go and step back from their role, to enable others to develop their SEN skills and expertise.

## The origin, concept and development of the teaching school

The forerunner's of the teaching school were the national support school (NSS) and the training school. Both types of school were the initiative of the previous Labour government. These two models of schools were extremely effective models for school-to-school support for improvement.

### National support schools

NSSs were schools and academies that were judged by OFSTED to be outstanding for overall effectiveness, leadership and management, the capacity to improve and had a consistent three-year upward trend in pupil attainment and progress. These schools were designed to provide integrated support and help to those schools facing challenging circumstances, and who were underperforming below the Department for Children, Schools and Families (DCSF) and now DfE floor standards. The NSSs were tasked by the DCSF/DfE to turn around struggling schools. These schools often had an outstanding headteacher who had taken on the role of a national leader of education (NLE), providing school-to-school leadership support in the form of becoming the executive headteacher, working in the underachieving school until it had improved and recruited a new headteacher. In addition to the headteacher of the NSS taking on leadership responsibilities beyond their own school, the NSS acting or associate headteacher, along with other key senior and middle leaders, such as the SENCO, would also provide outreach support to the school in challenging circumstances.

The underperforming partner school also had the opportunity to visit the NSS in order to observe outstanding and good practice at leadership and classroom level. The NSS would also provide coaching and mentoring for new or inexperienced staff at the partner school, in addition to support with joint teacher planning, and facilitating individual or group training.

A local leader of education (LLE) programme for outstanding headteachers was subsequently launched, following the NLE model. However, the former programme was different, in that it did not require the LLE to go and take on an executive headteacher role in the underperforming school. The LLE model entailed coaching and mentoring leaders and supporting a leadership development programme.

### Training schools

Training schools in England were officially designated with this status by the DCSF, under the previous Labour government. They focused on developing and delivering high-quality initial teacher training (ITT). Training schools provide exceptional facilities for INSET and work experience placements for trainee teachers. These schools acted as a centre of excellence for high-quality professional development for newly qualified and serving teachers.

The training schools placed trainee teachers in paired or multiple placements, working closely with higher education (HE) institutions, the LA, and other local schools and academies. Two-hundred-and-forty training schools have been operating across England, and the coalition government has succeeded in bringing together the training school and teaching school models to create a national network of teaching schools.

### Teaching schools

Teaching schools were introduced by the coalition government in 2011 as an outcome from their White Paper in 2010 entitled *The Importance of Teaching*. This DfE document stated:

> The network of Teaching Schools will include the very best schools with outstanding and innovative practice, in teaching and learning and significant experience developing teachers' professional practice. These schools are best placed to lead system-wide improvement in an area.
>
> (DfE 2010b: 7.8)

The current government envisages that there will be 500 teaching schools across England in the academic year 2014–2015.

Teaching schools, which are outstanding schools, are led by outstanding headteachers, many of whom are either NLEs or LLEs.

The concept and key purpose of the teaching school is to identify and draw upon the great practice existing across their alliance (partner) schools. This enables partner leaders and other outstanding staff to disseminate and share their expertise and skills with other schools in need of significant improvement, to improve the quality of their professional practice and improve pupil attainment. In order to become a teaching school, the following criteria must be met:

- evidence of successful collaborative work with other schools;
- outstanding OFSTED inspection judgements for overall effectiveness, teaching and learning, and leadership and management;
- consistently high levels of pupil performance and continued improvement;
- an outstanding headteacher with three or more years' leadership experience;
- outstanding senior and middle leaders with the capacity to support others in other schools, and to deliver high quality teacher training, CPD and school-to-school support.

Teaching schools have three core roles, which include:

1  To provide support for trainee teachers, leaders and other colleagues in schools.
2  To provide support for schools facing challenging circumstances, e.g. below the DfE floor standards and in an OFSTED category such as special measures or required improvement.
3  To contribute to the wider system through collaborative work to create a network of schools (an alliance), that works in partnership to deliver one or two in the above list of core roles.

Steve Mumby, Chief Executive of the National College for School Leadership (NCSL), commented in the Foreword of the NCSL document entitled *National Teaching School Prospectus* (3rd edition):

> Teaching schools will play a fundamental role in the future of school improvement, ITT, CPD and leadership development in this country. They will provide the impetus, co-ordination and focus that is so critical to achieving excellence through learning from and working with others.
>
> (NCSL 2012b)

Any type of educational setting can apply to become a teaching school, providing that they meet the criteria for designation. Secondary phase teaching schools with their alliance schools can work with between fifteen to twenty schools. Primary phase teaching schools with their alliance schools can work with between fifty to sixty partner schools, including special schools. Teaching schools take a leading role in brokering school-to-school support, a role previously undertaken by the local authority.

The NCSL is responsible for delivering the teaching school's programme, in partnership with the Teaching Agency, previously known at the Training and Development Agency for Schools (TDA). The NCSL is also taking a lead in the quality assurance of teaching schools, and it has the power to remove teaching school designation, which is for four years, from any teaching school not meeting the expected standards. The DfE in the Green Paper entitled *Support and Aspiration: A New Approach to Special Educational Needs and Disability* commented on teaching schools:

> The Teaching Schools network will play a proactive role in brokering partnerships between schools, quality assuring and supporting high calibre professional development for school staff.
>
> (DfE 2011c: 3.16)

The DfE in the same Green Paper goes on to remark:

> Teaching School partnerships will provide an excellent way for local areas to develop specialists, for example in behaviour and emotional support, who are able to work across school clusters, including with and between special schools.
>
> (DfE 2011c: 3.17)

Outstanding SENCOs clearly have an important role to play in teaching schools, especially if they are an SLE, which is explored in greater depth in this book in Chapter 2. Teaching schools play a key role in the deployment of SLEs.

Teaching schools may also be responsible for delivering two very effective programmes, which develop teachers' professional skills and expertise. These are the outstanding teacher programme (OTP) and the improving teacher programme (ITP).

### The outstanding teacher programme

The outstanding teacher programme (OTP) was first delivered as part of the Labour government's City Challenge initiative. The OTP comprises a ten-session, school-based course aimed at enabling good teachers to become outstanding, and gain the skills with which to assist other teachers in raising their performance. The training sessions are a combination of face-to-face learning and in-school practice. The OTP offers a proven process for developing excellence in effective and reflective teachers who can deliver and model excellent teaching and learning. The course includes developing and practising coaching skills, and exploring teaching and learning methodology. To engage with the OTP the headteacher must nominate the teachers who meet the following criteria:

- three years' teaching experience;
- shows evidence of pupils making progress;
- has an improving trend in pupil test or examination results;
- shows evidence of attending regular relevant professional development;
- uses pupil feedback to evaluate their own teaching and improve their practice;
- is a highly respected inspiring professional who demonstrates high order interpersonal skills, and is a positive role model to pupils and staff;
- shows a commitment to their own CPD and that of others.

The OTP may appeal to those SENCOs early on in their career, who would prefer to become a teaching leader, developing their own SEN team within their own educational setting.

### The improving teacher programme

The improving teacher programme (ITP) gives teachers a set of skills and strategies to reach the next teaching level. The programme is targeted at those teachers aspiring to deliver consistently good lessons.

The ITP consists of six facilitated face-to-face sessions over a five-to-six-week period. The programme covers: an introduction to teaching and learning; lesson starters and plenaries; assessment; differentiation; questioning; and putting the theory of effective teaching and learning into practice by teaching two lessons to a group of pupils.

### Teaching leaders

The teaching leader programme was first launched in 2008 under the Labour government. It has been so successful that it continues to be offered through the NCSL. The programme is designed for middle leaders new to the role who are working in a challenging school, where there are at least twenty per cent of pupils on free school meals (FSM), and whole school standards are judged to be below the government's floor standards. A new SENCO in the early years of middle leadership, who wishes to lead improvement within their own school, may be interested in pursuing such a course, providing they meet the eligibility criteria:

- at least up to three years' or more experience of middle leadership;
- strong teaching ability, evidenced by OFSTED during inspection;
- a passion for improvement;
- a desire to develop themselves professionally, as well as others in their team or department;
- possess good analytical and strategic thinking skills;
- can commit the time required to complete the teaching leader training in two years, with a guaranteed non-contact period per week in school for study.

The SENCO would have to remain working in their current educational setting for the two-year duration of the programme. The teaching leader course comprises of formal training, coaching and support, and an improvement initiative that is undertaken by the trainee teaching leader back in their own school. This improvement initiative must have an impact on pupil outcomes.

There are five key stages that middle leaders undertaking the teaching leader programme must experience. These are illustrated and explained in Table 1.3.

*Table 1.3* The five stages of the teaching leader learning journey

| EXPLORE | EMBARK | EXTEND | EMBED | EMPOWER |
|---|---|---|---|---|
| 1 Audit of SEN in own school. <br> 2 Review own leadership skills. <br> 3 Plan your improvement initiative for SEN. | 1 Launch your improvement initiative for SEN in your school. <br> 2 Test your hypotheses. <br> 3 Monitor pupil and team performance. | 1 Evaluate your impact to date. <br> 2 Deepen your focus. <br> 3 Innovate, based on your learning so far. | 1 Systemise your interventions. <br> 2 Communicate your learning and achievements across the SEN team or department. | 1 Transfer your skills to others. <br> 2 Plan for SEN change on a school-wide level. |

(Adapted from Teaching Leaders 2011, participant experience)

---

## Points to remember

- Outstanding schools can convert to academy status and, like free schools, they are independent from local authority control.
- There is now only one single early years setting and school-based category for SEN, replacing Action and Action Plus.
- IEPs are not required by those children and young people on a single education, health and care plan (EHCP).
- SEN policies need to be simplified and downsized, and written in parent-friendly language.
- Her Majesty's Inspectors (HMIs) in school and academy OFSTED inspections will be exploring SEND.
- Teaching schools play a major role in leading school-to-school improvement.
- Opportunities exist for outstanding SENCOs to explore becoming either a teaching leader or a specialist leader of education.
- SENCOs need to be reviewing their job description to reflect the new changes, which broaden their wider role beyond their own school.

---

## Further activities for reflection

1   In light of the latest changes in the SEN system, what will be your first priority as a SENCO in your own educational setting?
2   What are the implications for your SENCO role, in the context of your own educational setting, if you become an SLE or teaching leader?
3   What further professional development do you require to prepare you for your changing SENCO role, particularly if working in an outreach capacity?
4   What do you see as being the benefits of pooling some funding with a cluster of schools in a local area, in order to secure additional services for SEN pupils?
5   How will the changes in the SEN system influence and affect the role of teaching assistants in your educational setting, and how will you manage this situation?
6   How do you envisage academies and free schools fitting in with the new SEN system, and what would these educational settings contribute to the local SENCO network and partnership?

# Chapter 2

# School-to-school support for SEND

---

**This chapter covers:**

- The concept of school-to-school support
- Models of school-to-school support for improvement in SEND
- The leadership characteristics required by SENCOs engaging in school-to-school support for SEND
- The SENCO as a specialist leader of education
- Strategies a SENCO will use in improving underperforming schools in SEND
- Cameos of good practice illustrating school-to-school support for SEND

---

## The concept of school-to-school support

School-to-school support entails recognising the importance of connections between different issues, individuals and institutions, to encourage collaboration between schools, in order to remove educational disadvantage for those pupils with SEND, and who are on free school meals (FSM).

The DfE in their White Paper *The Importance of Teaching* commented:

> We know that teachers learn best from other professionals and that an 'open classroom' culture is vital.
>
> (DfE 2010b: 2.4)

Effective inter-school support, based on coaching and mentoring, does improve the quality of leadership and teaching.

The concept of school-to-school support has been delivered through clusters of schools, which may be of the same phase, faith group or a secondary school with feeder primary schools, all geographically based. More recently, the term family of schools, and the teaching school alliance, are taking a lead role in the delivery of school-to-school improvement support in the 21st century. Not every school has to be in a cluster, for example, free schools.

A self-improving school system (SISS), according to David Hargreaves, has developed as a result of the diminishing centralisation of government and local authorities in relation to leading school improvement, with outstanding school leaders, as NLEs and LLEs, and other outstanding senior and middle leaders, which includes outstanding SENCOs, taking the lead role in school improvement. As schools become self-improving and self-managing, and far less reliant on the local authority (LA), families of schools and school clusters take on the middle tier role that was previously the LA role.

School improvement clusters of schools and families of schools accept collective responsibility for self-improvement, for the cluster as a whole, and not just for their own school. In order that a SISS is effective, four main features are required:

### 1 Capitalising on the benefits of clusters, networks and families of schools

Good practice and resources are shared with other schools in the cluster or family of schools, and mutual school visits (learning walks) take place. For example, an outstanding special school or mainstream school, within the cluster or family of schools, will share their SEND expertise between the schools, to help build capacity in SEND. They will also work with a weaker school on SEND, in or beyond the cluster group or family of schools, to improve that aspect, whole school, in the partner school.

### 2 Adopting a local solution approach

A local solution approach involves local self-evaluation, local objectives and local action plans. Schools in the cluster or family of schools work together to identify the problems and devise solutions, tailored to local circumstances and resources. For example, there may be an issue existing locally, relating to the families of children with SEND or on FSM, which identifies that these families would benefit from a Family Support Worker. The cluster or family of schools are able to pool some of their collective funding, such as the pupil premium money, to fund a Family Support Worker, who can then work across a group of schools, with targeted families in the local area.

### 3 Stimulating co-construction between schools

For example, clusters and families of schools agree upon the nature of a collective SEND task: they set priorities, co-design action plans, and view their implementation as a co-production, i.e. a collaborative and collective responsibility. This co-construction is the action taken to ensure what works well in particular contexts, which is adapted, adjusted and transferred to other schools within the cluster or family of schools, in order to achieve the expected outcomes. For example, a cluster of schools may agree to implement Achievement for All (AfA) across all schools in need of improvement in SEND, or implement a particular intervention programme that raises SEND pupils' attainment in literacy, such as Better Reading.

### 4 Expanding the concept of system leadership

System leadership at all levels involves effective senior or middle leaders, including outstanding SENCOs, who may be an SLE, working with other schools, in the cluster or family of schools, to improve pupil outcomes, particularly those of SEND and FSM children. At the heart of successful school-to-school partnership working lies three core features. These are:

1 **Co-ordination**, consensus building relating to roles and responsibilities, ways of working and partnership goals.
2 **Communication**, information sharing and being open and honest with each other.
3 **Bonding**, where staff enjoy working together and trust each other.

The principles of school-to-school support for SEND:

- To close the attainment gap between different pupil groups, which includes those with SEND.
- To make a difference for all pupils, but particularly those with SEND.
- To transform the partner school culture, in being successful in meeting the needs of SEND pupils in an inclusive school.

- To ensure the quality of teaching and learning for SEND pupils is at least consistently good across the partner school, but preferably as a longer-term goal, for the quality to become consistently outstanding.
- To use the most appropriate improvement strategies that give 'quick wins' for SEND, whole school, in the partner school.

## Models of school-to-school support for improvement in SEND

Different models of partnership working between schools exist, and the SENCO who is providing school-to-school support for SEND will need to be familiar with the different types of collaborations, in order to understand the different contexts they may work within.

**Single school** – who does not engage with any formal or informal collaborations.

**Partnerships** – formal and informal groups of schools and academies agree to work together.

**Collaborations** – a formal partnership that establishes a strategic group across the partnership.

**Trusts** – a strategic partnership encompassing one or more schools, with partners from outside education, who all deliver improved outcomes.

**Federations** – a formal structure of two or more schools, governed collectively under a single governing body.

**Academies** – these can be sponsored or converting academies. They are both independent of the local authority, and both may be part of multi-academy trusts or chains. They utilise innovative leadership structures to help them tackle underachievement. Converting academies have to work with other schools to help raise standards.

**Mixed federations and collaborations** – this entails utilising collaborative arrangements for both models in order to establish a strategic group across the partnership.

**Free schools** – funded in the same way as academies, and are independent of local authority control. Sponsorship of free schools is usually by teachers, parents, community groups and others.

### Teaching school partnership models

**Alliance** – a teaching school works together with other local schools (alliances) to deliver training and CPD to teachers, support staff and headteachers. Together, they raise standards through school-to-school support. An alliance can be cross-phase, cross-LA or cross-region.

**Strategic partners** – some members of a teaching school alliance may be strategic partners who take responsibility for some of the teaching school's delivery. For example, they may be other schools, a university partner or an organisation.

**Network** – this comprises of a number of teaching school alliances working together to form a network to share services and knowledge.

**Job share** – two schools or academies may become a teaching school, job sharing the teaching school work and responsibilities, but each school or academy must individually meet the teaching school eligibility criteria.

## The leadership characteristics required by SENCOs engaging in school-to-school support for SEND

Some or all of the following leadership characteristics are generally observed among SENCOs engaging in school-to-school improvement.

- A successful motivator of others, to give their best to SEND pupils.
- A confident modeller of good practice in the teaching of SEND pupils.
- Values and respects diversity in other SENCOs and teachers, building on their strengths and talents.
- Inspirational, yet convincing, in empowering others to take responsibility for SEND pupils.
- Knowledgeable about other local schools', networks' and organisations' SEND provision, and adapt this to the immediate partner school context.
- Driven by a commitment to improving the life chances of SEND pupils.
- Successful in building trusting relationships with the SENCO and staff in the partner school they are supporting.
- Resilient to challenging situations, persevering in improving SEND in a partner school, against all odds.
- Willing to learn from the partner school context, and takes the time to understand the partner school's culture and ways of working.

## The SENCO as a specialist leader of education

The concept of an SLE was first introduced by the DfE in their White Paper (2010b) *The Importance of Teaching*, which commented:

> We will also designate 'Specialist Leaders of Education' – excellent professionals in leadership positions below the headteacher (such as deputies, bursars, heads of department) who will support others in similar positions in other schools.
>
> (DfE 2010b: 2.26)

Similarly, the DfE in their Green Paper (2011c), *Support and Aspiration: A New Approach to Special Educational Needs and Disabilities*, commented on SLEs:

> We will create a new designation of Specialist Leaders of Education. These will be serving middle and senior school leaders who are outstanding at what they do and who are able to play a role beyond their school, supporting others to improve, including those who work with children with SEN and disabilities.
>
> (DfE 2011c: 3.22)

The SLEs are senior and middle leaders from all types of schools, operating at all levels, who demonstrate a high standard of expertise and a commitment to supporting other schools to improve. SLEs do not have to come from an outstanding school. They can be drawn from any school working in a teaching school alliance, which includes a national support school or a school where the headteacher is an LLE. They promote a system-wide culture of leadership and school improvement. SLEs are, however, closely linked to the teaching school vision, as they may be deployed to support an NLE or other leader, who is an executive headteacher, supporting an underperforming school. SLEs are expected to be highly accomplished leaders of what they do, and they have to have a strong track record in coaching and facilitation skills in bringing on and developing other colleagues.

The first cohort of 1,000 SLEs took up their posts in the opening years of 2012. The DfE envisage there will be 5,000 SLEs in operation by 2014, working alongside a network of 500 teaching schools. Teaching schools will deliver the SLE training programme. They will also designate SLEs using the NCSL criteria, and will help schools to find the SLE that is appropriate for them. Teaching schools will also maintain a directory of expertise, which schools can consult to find the SLE to help them with their particular issue or challenge.

SLEs bring together all the great work that classroom specialists have been doing in schools, acting as a leadership link between the classroom and the leadership team.

*The role of specialist leaders of education*

SLEs working beyond their own school will undertake the following roles, which have been identified in the NCSL *Specialist Leaders of Education Prospectus*:

- one-to-one support;
- facilitated group support;
- use and analysis of data;
- diagnosis of strengths and areas for development.

(NCSL 2011d: 3)

SLEs also support the professional development of leaders in the partner school they are supporting. For example, the SLE with SEN expertise (an outstanding SENCO) will be working with the senior leadership team, including the SENCO in the school requiring support to improve SEND.

The SENCO who is an SLE may also be commissioned by a teaching school to undertake research, in an area of SEND, which will help to inform local or national policymakers.

The criteria for becoming a specialist leader of education are:

- outstanding middle or senior leader with at least two years' experience of leadership, with high levels of knowledge in the particular area of expertise;
- have a successful track record of working with a range of leaders within their own and/or another school;
- evidence of using coaching and/or facilitation skills to bring about sustainable improvements in the area of expertise;
- committed to undertaking outreach work, and balance this with their own school work;
- have excellent communication and interpersonal skills;
- emotionally intelligent and sensitive in working with others collaboratively;
- understanding of what 'outstanding' in their field entails, and able to articulate this to help others achieve outstanding in the partner school;
- appreciate how their specialism and skills contribute to the wider school improvement agenda;
- analytical skills in identifying priorities and needs, with the ability to set and establish new and innovative ways of working;
- the ability to grow leadership capacity in others;
- able to give up fifteen days per year to SLE work.

## Areas of expertise of specialist leaders of education

The directory of SLE expertise has been organised in the NCSL *SLE Prospectus*, under the four OFSTED school and academy inspection aspects. These are illustrated in Table 2.1.

*Table 2.1* Specialist leaders of education areas of expertise

| Key area | Area of expertise |
| --- | --- |
| Leadership and management | Academies/academy transition and conversion<br>Federations<br>Leadership of CPD<br>Networks, partnerships and collaboration<br>Quality standards<br>School business management/financial management<br>Self-evaluation<br>Strategic analysis/diagnostics<br>Subject/key stage/phase/faculty leadership and management<br>Teams, staffing, restructures and performance management |
| Pupil achievement | Assessment for Learning (AfL)/tracking pupil progress/data<br>Closing the gap with a focus on FSM and vulnerable groups<br>Curriculum development<br>English as an additional language (EAL)<br>Early years<br>English<br>Geography<br>History<br>Literacy<br>Maths<br>Modern foreign language (MFL)<br>Mobility<br>Numeracy<br>Other subject areas, e.g. ICT<br>Phonics<br>Science<br>SEN<br>Sixth forms<br>Support for the most able pupils |
| Quality of teaching | Teaching and learning<br>Initial teacher training (ITT) and newly qualified teachers (NQTs) |
| Behaviour and safety | Safeguarding learners<br>Behaviour/discipline<br>Attendance<br>Pupil leadership/voice |

(Source: NCSL 2011d: 16, *Specialist Leaders of Education Prospectus*)

## The benefits of becoming an SLE for SENCOs

There are a number of benefits for a SENCO taking on the role of an SLE. These are outlined below.

- Strengthens collaborative working.
- Offers opportunities to work creatively and try out new ideas.
- Further strengthens the SLE's coaching and facilitation skills.
- Broadens the SLE's knowledge of working in different contexts.
- Opportunity to learn from others, and further improve own performance.
- Offers good networking opportunities with other peers.
- Offers greater opportunity for autonomy in working.
- Personal reward in knowing that the SLE is helping to improve SEN pupils' outcomes.

## Strategies a SENCO will use in improving underperforming schools in SEND

An outstanding SENCO as an SLE is likely to utilise a range of improvement strategies at two levels: whole school and targeted pupil level.

### Whole school strategies for improvement in SEND

A SENCO as an SLE will be working with senior leaders in the partner school to:

- improve the consistency of high-quality first teaching (QFT) and learning across the school, supported by CPD in SEND, lesson observations, moderation of teacher assessment and coaching;
- support targeted class teachers to personalise and tailor the curriculum to engage SEND pupils in appropriate and relevant learning experiences;
- model the use of appropriate assessment for SEND pupils, in order to enable class teachers to track, monitor and analyse pupil performance each term, judging progress against the relevant national datasets in the *Progression Guidance*;
- support teachers in developing high-quality learning environments, which consistently support SEND children's learning, as well as promote access to learning resources;
- ensure that teachers being supported consistently follow the school's rewards and sanctions system, and behaviour and attendance policies, with SEND pupils;
- support the senior leadership team and the SEND governor in maintaining their vision and ambition for SEND pupils, in order to raise staff expectations.

### Targeted pupil-level strategies for improvement in SEND

The targeted pupil-level strategies help:

- support teachers' early identification of pupils with SEND, accompanied with appropriate learning interventions, which help to close the attainment gap;
- advise on one-to-one and/or catch-up provision for SEND pupils, which should be delivered by suitably qualified and skilled staff;
- support the development of the SENCO's monitoring and evaluation skills, in order to enable them to judge the impact of additional support and interventions on SEND pupils' progress and attainment;
- support teachers and the SENCO, where necessary, in how to work productively and positively with the parents of SEND children, to help them support their child's learning, behaviour and personal development;
- advise the senior leaders to provide SEND children with a key adult, who will act as a mentor and pastoral guide;
- advise the SENCO on the effective management of key transitions for SEND pupils between phases, key stages, year groups, schools and colleges.

The SENCO in the role of an SLE may wish to use Table 2.2 to record and monitor the activities and support they deliver to a school requiring improvement in SEN.

*Table 2.2* Record sheet for SLE school-to-school support in SEN

| Nature of SLE support and intervention for SEN | Monitoring SLE support | Impact and outcomes of SLE support |
|---|---|---|
| | | |
| | | |
| | | |
| | | |
| | | |
| | | |
| | | |
| | | |
| | | |

 *Promoting and Delivering School-to-School Support for Special Educational Needs*, Routledge © Rita Cheminais 2013

## Cameos of good practice illustrating school-to-school support for SEND

### Cameo 1

An outstanding infant school, on the retirement of the headteacher, moved from outstanding school status, to one in need of improvement. The school SENCO took early retirement, and the newly appointed headteacher allocated the SENCO role to the deputy headteacher. The local authority advised the headteacher to commission the support of an outstanding SENCO from a local teaching school.

This SENCO undertook a whole school audit, which identified SEN areas for improvement. An action plan was developed, and ongoing support and guidance continued to be delivered by the outstanding SENCO, who coached the deputy headteacher. The outstanding SENCO helped to support the school in setting up a manageable system for identifying, registering, monitoring and reviewing SEND pupil progress. She also delivered a whole school INSET on meeting the needs of SEND pupils, which helped to raise teacher expectations and build capacity in the school's support workforce. The progress and attainment of children with SEND is beginning to improve across the infant school.

### Cameo 2

A group of three rural primary schools, within a locality, agreed to share an outstanding SENCO. The SENCO worked for one-and-a-half days in each school and spent half a day (Friday afternoons) reviewing the impact of her work. The SENCO agreed with the three headteachers that she would focus on her strategic role in each school, while helping to build greater capacity for SEND, among the class teachers and teaching assistants. To make best use of the SENCO, the schools pooled some of their CPD budget to enable the SENCO to deliver a programme of twilight SEND sessions to all the staff at the three schools, on the same evening, at the end of the school day, each half term. The topics covered included QFT; analysing and using SEND pupil-level data to inform improvement; SEND pupil-centred reviews; productive partnership working with parents of SEND pupils; and meeting the OFSTED SEND expectations. The SENCO's weekly visits to each school entailed her undertaking lesson observations; classroom walkthroughs; holding a weekly SEND drop-in lunchtime session for staff at the school; meeting with the SEND governor at least once a term; and feeding back to the headteacher after each weekly visit. She would also keep the provision map under review, and monitor the impact of additional interventions undertaken by SEND pupils. At the end of the summer term, the SENCO organised a SEND showcase event, which celebrated the work of the three schools, and their partner services, in helping to improve the achievements and well-being of SEND children.

### Cameo 3

A secondary school located in an area of high social deprivation was identified by OFSTED, through its inspection process, of not enabling SEND pupils to make good enough progress, in relation to their age and starting point, on entry to the school. The school's SENCO, shortly after the inspection, went off sick with stress. The headteacher, on the advice of the local authority, commissioned an outstanding SENCO who was an SLE in SEND from another local secondary school, to coach and mentor a teacher in the learning support department to take on the SENCO role temporarily. The SLE, with the support of the SLT in the school requiring improvement, undertook paired classroom walkthroughs with the learning support teacher across the school where SEND pupils were making least progress. Both fed back on their observations to each other and to the SLT in the school, and two top SEND priorities were identified: assessing SEND pupil progress and curriculum differentiation. The SLE arranged for the Learning Support Teacher taking on the SENCO role temporarily to observe high-quality inclusive teaching in their school. This enabled the learning support teacher from the improving school to observe first hand how best to meet the learning needs of SEND pupils across the curriculum, and the type of learning resources that successfully enhanced curriculum access.

The SLE met with the heads of department at the improving school to help support them in building on the existing good practice for SEND in the school, and to further raise SEND pupils' attainment and progress through making the curriculum more accessible and using more appropriate assessments for learning. Heads of department, where improvement was needed in the subject area, were paired up with another good or outstanding head of department of the same subject area in the SLE's own school. Together, they worked on improving curriculum differentiation and moderating SEND pupils' work, to help validate the accuracy of teacher assessment in the improving school.

The SLE signposted the headteacher and the teacher from the learning support department in the improving school to appropriate SEND training from an external credible education consultant. The SLE did agree to deliver some demonstration lessons to those teachers who were identified as needing the most help and support in raising the attainment of SEND pupils. This was followed up by a series of mentoring sessions on the 'craft of teaching' to enhance SEND pupils' learning opportunities.

After two terms of input from the SLE, SEND pupil attainment and progress began to make some improvement in those subject departments targeted for further support.

---

### Points to remember

- School-to-school support is a collaborative process, designed to promote a culture of professional learning among teachers, in order to close the attainment gap of vulnerable pupils, which includes those with SEND.
- A self-improving school system has arisen as a result of the diminishing role of the local authority in leading and supporting school improvement.
- There are three essential core features at the heart of successful school-to-school partnership working. These are: coordination, communication and bonding.
- There are many different models of school-to-school support.
- Outstanding SENCOs, with a successful track record in supporting other schools with SEND, should apply to become a specialist leader of education.
- SENCOs, as SLEs supporting another school in the improvement of SEND policy and provision, need to utilise improvement strategies at two levels: whole school and targeted pupil level.

---

### Further activities for reflection

1   Of the experiences you have had already of working as a SENCO beyond your own school, what were the benefits of your input for the other school?
2   If you were commissioned to support another SENCO in an underperforming school, what would be your first priority in developing a productive professional working partnership?
3   If you were asked to turn around SEND policy and provision in another school, what support would you expect to enable you to perform your role effectively?
4   What approaches would you use when working with a SENCO in another school who is resistant to change for improvement in SEND?
5   How would you ensure that the work you do to support another school does not compromise SEND standards in your own school?
6   In your view, how can school-to-school support for SEND effectively replace the school improvement role of the local authority?

# Chapter 3

# Leading the implementation of Achievement for All

**This chapter covers:**

- Background to Achievement for All
- Outcomes from the Achievement for All pilot project
- Introduction to managing the change process for Achievement for All
- Top tips and practical strategies for SENCOs managing change for the Achievement for All programme
- Implementing the Achievement for All programme
- The role of teachers engaging with the Achievement for All programme
- Key questions for schools engaging with Achievement for All
- How schools used the Achievement for All funding in the pilot project

## Background to Achievement for All

The Achievement for All (AfA) project was piloted from September 2009 to September 2011 in ten local authorities across England (Bexley, Camden, Coventry, East Sussex, Essex, Gloucestershire, Nottingham, Oldham, Redcar and Cleveland, and Sheffield). There were 454 maintained schools involved in the project, which was the initiative of the Labour government, in partnership with the National Strategies and the National College for School Leadership (NCSL). SEND pupils in Years 1, 5, 7 and 10 were targeted at all stages on the SEN Code of Practice.

AfA adopts a whole school approach to school improvement, focusing on outcomes rather than processes, offering a framework that can be tailored to suit the context of the school or academy, to raise the aspirations, access and achievement of SEND pupils and other vulnerable groups. The SEND Green Paper (2011c) commented on AfA:

> Achievement for All has shown that the engagement of effective school leadership, high expectations, greater and more constructive involvement of parents, clear target setting and careful tracking of pupils' progress leads to an improvement in the outcomes pupils achieve – including improvements for those children and young people who have experienced barriers to learning.
>
> (DfE 2011c: 3.29)

It goes on to add:

> The Achievement for All programme has led to schools declassifying children previously identified at School Action, because with a culture of high expectations and provision of personalised school-based support the label itself is no longer necessary.
>
> (DfE 2011c: 3.30)

Brian Lamb, OBE in the Lamb Inquiry report from 2009, made the recommendation that the Achievement for All work should be sustained after the two-year pilot, disseminating good practice and materials more widely, beyond the pilot schools.

Achievement for All has three core objectives. These aim to improve:

- the achievement and progress of SEND children and young people;
- the engagement of parents of SEND children and young people with their child's school;
- the wider outcomes of children and young people with SEND.

In order to enable a school to achieve these core objectives, they must engage with originally three main strands and now a fourth strand on leadership, which was added after the pilot project was completed. The four strands of AfA are as follows:

1   **Assessment, tracking and intervention** – high QFT and learning opportunities within and beyond the classroom, leading to improved progress for SEND pupils, through high expectations, effective use of AfL, assessing pupil progress (APP) and focused target setting.
2   **Structured conversation with parents** – to be held once a term, led by the class teacher or SENCO, focusing on four aspects: explore, focus, plan and review.
3   **Provision for developing wider outcomes** – whole school strategies to support pupils to make progress in any two of the following areas: attendance, behaviour, bullying, positive relationships and increasing participation.
4   **Leadership of Achievement for All** – whole school leadership, with leaders at all levels taking collective responsibility for AfA. Effective leaders of AfA, according to the NCSL, have the following characteristics:
    - a clear core purpose and vision for educational provision in support of vulnerable learners, particularly those with SEND;
    - secure a commitment from all staff in the school to the vision that all pupils can succeed;
    - work in collaboration and are accountable to improve outcomes for SEND pupils;
    - effective in communicating the message that all pupils, at whatever starting point, need or ability, will increase access and raise achievement within a culture of high aspiration.

(NCSL 2011a: 18)

Those schools which have or are engaging with AfA are well placed in relation to meeting the latest OFSTED inspection requirements, which strengthens the focus on parental engagement, the achievement of SEND pupils and the extent to which these pupils are making progress.

The coalition government would like to see AfA implemented in all maintained schools in England. However, there is a cost element for those schools wishing to engage in the AfA process, which has the potential to lead to a Quality Mark. The cost per year is based on the size of the school/number of pupils, which can range from £3,000 to £6,000 per year, with matched funding from the DfE.

A school or academy may decide to engage with AfA, without wishing to work towards gaining the Quality Mark, where there are budget constraints. The school or academy can simply download the two DfE Achievement for All reports and the DCSF original Guidance for schools, all of which are free, using these throughout the AfA journey to support implementation. An external 'critical friend' from another AfA school could monitor progress towards implementation.

## Outcomes from the Achievement for All pilot project

The DfE document following up on their SEND Green Paper on progress and next steps, commented on their intention, which is to:

expand the Achievement for All programme which has led to significant improvements in academic and wider outcomes for pupils with SEN.

(DfE 2012: 3.3)

Later in Chapter 3 of the same document, the DfE commented:

> We are building lessons from Achievement for All into teacher and school leadership training.
>
> (DfE 2012: 3.14)

AfA has been most successful when schools build on their existing good practice, and share their good practice with other schools. Successful implementation of AfA took place in those schools where there was strong leadership for the initiative from the headteacher, or the senior leadership team, who took the burden for whole school implementation away from the SENCO. Only eighteen per cent of schools in the initial pilot for AfA assigned the SENCO or Inclusion Manager to lead the programme whole school. AfA was considered to enable every teacher in the school to acknowledge that SEND pupils were their responsibility within the inclusive classroom, and that they were expected to make progress. The final evaluation of the Achievement for All pilot project was published by the DfE in November 2011. Some of the key findings from the report revealed that:

- 37 per cent of AfA SEND pupils achieved or exceeded expected levels of progress in English, compared to all pupils nationally;
- 42 per cent of AfA SEND pupils achieved or exceeded expected levels of progress in Mathematics, compared to all pupils nationally;
- there was a 10 per cent drop in persistent absenteeism among AfA SEND pupils;
- there was 36 per cent improvement in excellent relationships with parents of AfA SEND children, including among 'hard to reach' parents;
- there was a drop in poor parental relationships in AfA schools from 11 per cent to 1.5 per cent;
- 90 per cent of the AfA schools in the pilot project intended to continue to use the structured conversations with parents of SEND pupils;
- There was improvement in AfA SEND pupils' behaviour, and a reduction in teacher-reported bullying and behaviour problems.

## Introduction to managing the change process for Achievement for All

Change, as an ongoing process, has a tendency to alter the status quo, challenge staff perceptions and promote reflective practice. Change is usually characterised by the desire to improve things, for example, improving SEND pupils' achievement and progress as a result of implementing the Achievement for All initiative. SENCOs, like other staff in the school or academy, are likely to experience an emotional journey. There are five stages in the emotional journey of change:

1  create a vision;
2  lead the change;
3  consult on the change;
4  engage stakeholders;
5  reflect on the change.

Communication throughout the change process is crucial, to ensure all stakeholders feel well-informed about the change developments. The Advisory, Conciliation and Arbitration Service (ACAS) offers a useful generic communications strategy checklist, which SENCOs and other senior leaders may find valuable to refer to.

- What is the issue?
- Who do I need to talk to?
- What do I need to say?
- How will I put across my message (strategy)?
- What methods will I use?
- How will I get feedback?

(ACAS 2010: 17)

Strong leadership is required by SENCOs, particularly if they are leading on the implementation of AfA. The features of strong leadership include:

- **Visibility** – doing classroom walkthroughs and making yourself accessible to staff, to gain a sense of the general mood for the AfA change.
- **Accessibility** – setting aside time to meet with members of the AfA team, including senior leaders, to keep them abreast of developments.
- **Consistency** – in sticking to the agreed AfA plan of action.
- **Decisiveness** – being able to make quick and firm decisions when necessary, explaining your reasons for making the decision.
- **Clarity** – about the AfA message (strategy), and communicating this effectively to other stakeholders.

## Top tips and practical strategies for SENCOs managing change for the Achievement for All programme

The SENCO will take on the role of change agent when they are leading on the implementation of AfA in their own school, or in another school requiring improvement in SEND. The following top ten tips are offered to support the SENCO in managing the change process.

1  Take time to understand the AfA initiative prior to implementation.
    Read previous reports on AfA and any government guidance. Also talk to other colleagues who have experience of implementing AfA, and share their positive views with staff in school.
2  Show courage and integrity in managing the change process for AfA.
    Staff will be less inclined to fight the change if they see the SENCO has the courage of their own convictions, and shows empathy and understanding about why some staff may be anxious about change. Where a SENCO shows integrity staff will trust them more to lead and manage the change process for AfA.
3  Engage and enthuse the staff affected by the change.
    Getting staff involved early in the AfA initiative and engaging positive role models who have experienced AfA will help to change those staff who may be sceptical or anxious about changing their classroom practice. Deal with any staff unrest upfront, and as soon as it arises, seeking the support of senior leaders where necessary.
4  Believe what staff do, rather than what they say.
    Some staff may tell the SENCO to their face that they are right behind them in supporting the implementation of AfA at a meeting but, in reality, they are delaying the implementation of AfA in their own classroom. The SENCO needs to find out why this might be happening and then convince these staff that AfA will work, by sharing evidence-based practice with them, taken from the DfE final evaluation report, or from staff in an AfA school nearby.
5  Act immediately as soon as anything begins to go wrong with the implementation of AfA.
    Some staff may not view AfA as a top priority, and begin to stop attending any AfA meetings. The SENCO needs to follow up on the lack of commitment, and offer coaching or mentoring for these teaching colleagues. If this does not resolve the issue, the SENCO should seek the support of the senior leadership team, to emphasise the value and importance of AfA in improving SEND pupils' achievement and progress.
6  Tweak the motivation system in the educational setting.
    For example, ensure the school's motivational system acknowledges collaborative teamwork within the organisation in successfully implementing the AfA initiative.
7  Utilise positive methods throughout the AfA journey.
    Staff are more likely to buy into AfA when a positive approach to change is adopted. The SENCO may use the appreciative inquiry as a way of enabling staff to be more open to change, and able to identify what works best in AfA.
8  Ensure there is no way back to the old ways for staff.
    The SENCO needs to give the staff in school an end date when they expect AfA embedded in everyday classroom practice. Regular monitoring of classroom practice across the school through walkthroughs can track where staff may be returning to their old ways or being complacent to change for AfA.

9  Don't be afraid to get help from the senior leadership team or an external professional. Effecting change poses a challenge for SENCOs, and it is important that they do not get bogged down with the problems of staff who do not comply with the AfA initiative. It is reasonable for the SENCO to seek further support from the SLT in school or, alternatively, from an external professional, performing the role of 'critical friend'.

10  Look after your well-being. Keep change management for AfA in perspective. Adopt a team approach, where together each achieves more, to avoid SENCO stress. Take time out to reflect and relax. Take regular exercise, have sufficient sleep and lead a healthy lifestyle outside work, in order to ensure the energy and enthusiasm for AfA is maintained by the SENCO, as lead change agent.

## Implementing the Achievement for All programme

The checklist below will offer a point of reference to those leading on the implementation of AfA.

- Form an AfA team, led by a member of the SLT or SENCO.
- Brief the key stakeholders on AfA.
- Carry out an audit to identify SEND strengths and areas for further improvement in relation to SEND pupils' attainment and progress.
- Using the findings from the audit, develop an AfA Action Plan which links in with the school development plan.
- Implement a monitoring cycle for assessing, tracking progress, identifying gaps, setting targets and implementing additional SEND provision for targeted SEND pupils, feeding back to the SLT and governors.
- Ensure class teachers or the SENCO hold structured conversations with parents of SEND pupils each term following the guidance provided.
- Ensure that two areas from the wider outcomes strand are implemented.
- Provide professional development for staff to support AfA.
- Ensure collaborative partnership working takes place with other partners to provide targeted interventions, and share best practice with other schools.
- Gather robust evidence throughout AfA implementation to evaluate impact and outcomes for targeted SEND pupils.
- Communicate the outcomes from the AfA programme to key stakeholders.
- Discuss with the SLT and the AfA team how the good practice can be sustained, year on year.

## The role of teachers engaging with the Achievement for All programme

The original guidance from the DCSF for implementing the Achievement for All programme expected class or subject teachers to do the following:

- assess, track and report each term on the progress of the targeted pupils;
- identify any gaps in the targeted pupils' learning;
- set ambitious targets for pupils to offer a good level of challenge;
- support the planning and implementation of appropriate interventions and strategies to make learning barrier-free and more accessible for pupils;
- hold a structured conversation with the parent(s) of each targeted pupil to discuss their child's achievements, progress and provision.

## Key questions for schools engaging with Achievement for All

The DCSF's *Achievement for All: Guidance for Schools*, published in September 2009, offered in paragraph 6.8 some suggested questions for schools engaging with AfA to consider.

- Are the targeted pupils making good progress and how do you know?
- Are expectations high enough and how do you know?
- Are curricular targets appropriate, do the pupils understand them and do they know how to achieve them?
- Have the Progression Materials 2010–2011 been used to support target setting and judgements about the progress of those pupils working well below age-related expectations?
- Where targeted pupils are working within P levels, how well are teacher assessments moderated and how appropriate are the set targets?
- Have the curriculum targets and information about steps of progression been shared with parents?
- Is teacher planning differentiated enough for targeted pupils to be actively engaged, enjoy their learning and make progress towards their targets in lessons?

(DCSF 2009c)

## How schools used the Achievement for All funding in the pilot project

AfA funding was used in a range of ways in the pilot project schools in 2009–2011, as illustrated in Table 3.1. Table 3.2 provides a tool to support an SLE in recording and reflecting on their AfA activities in another school.

*Table 3.1* Examples of how pilot schools used Achievement for All funding for two of the AfA strands

| Strand 1 – Assessment, tracking and intervention | Strand 3 – Wider outcomes |
| --- | --- |
| Providing additional intervention programmes for reading, e.g. Better Reading | Training a teaching assistant to deliver art therapy sessions to targeted pupils with emotional and behavioural difficulties |
| Training a teaching assistant to deliver speech and language programmes in small groups | Appointing a Family Support Worker to work with families under stress |
| Introducing 'Talking Partners' | Providing lunchtime and after-school clubs |
| Purchasing software to establish an Achievement for All tracking system, to monitor targeted pupils' progress across the curriculum | Providing workshops for pupils on anti-bullying, restorative justice and anger management |
| Employing an additional teacher to deliver one-to-one teaching for reading | Employing a Key Worker to provide tailored pastoral support and academic mentoring to targeted pupils |

*Table 3.2* Achievement for All learning log for a SENCO/SLE

| | What worked well? | What will you change? | What have you learnt? | Impact of activity? |
|---|---|---|---|---|
| Assessment, tracking and intervention | | | | |
| Structured conversation with parents of SEN pupils | | | | |
| Provision for developing SEN pupils' wider outcomes | | | | |
| Leadership of AfA | | | | |

**Points to remember**

- Achievement for All takes a whole school approach to school improvement with the key aim of improving outcomes for SEND pupils.
- The core objectives of Achievement for All are achieved by engaging with the four main strands: assessment, tracking and intervention; structured conversation with parents; provision for developing wider outcomes; and leadership.
- The four essential features of leadership for Achievement for All include: vision, commitment, collaboration and communication.
- Those organisations engaging with the Achievement for All programme are at an advantage in the OFSTED inspection.
- It is important to facilitate the involvement of staff as early as possible in the Achievement for All change process.
- Change is characterised by the desire to improve things.

**Further activities for reflection**

1   What is your school's current position in relation to the four strands of Achievement for All?
2   What opportunities do you envisage Achievement for All would bring to your school?
3   What would be your first change management priority if you were asked to lead on the implementation of Achievement for All in your school?
4   What strategies would you utilise to tackle teacher complacency about Achievement for All?
5   How will you measure your Achievement for All change management progress?

# Chapter 4

# Making best use of the pupil premium

---

**This chapter covers:**

- The origin, concept and principles of the pupil premium
- Those who benefit from the pupil premium
- The amount of pupil premium allocated to disadvantaged children
- How to make effective use of the pupil premium
- Monitoring and evaluating the impact of the pupil premium
- Validating best practice in the pupil premium

---

## The origin of the pupil premium

The concept of the pupil premium originated in the USA in 1970, where the poorer children received a supplementary voucher. The idea for a similar voucher scheme was proposed by Professor Julian Le Grand in the UK in 1989. The professor continued to write about the topic for the next twenty years. The Liberal Democrats began to think about the idea for the pupil premium in 2001, eventually seeing the policy endorsed by Nick Clegg in 2007. The Conservative government favoured Professor Le Grand's original idea of a pupil's background determining the degree of financial help they would receive to support their education. In 2008, the Policy Exchange published its report entitled *School Funding and Social Justice: A Guide to the Pupil Premium* (Freedman and Horner 2008). This report was significant in enabling the coalition government to implement the pupil premium, from 1st April 2011.

## The concept of the pupil premium

The concept of the pupil premium in the era of the coalition government is to help close the attainment gap between poor disadvantaged children and their more social and economically advantaged peers, by allocating additional funding in order to enhance their life changes and future opportunities.

The Education Secretary Michael Gove commented in July 2010, during the launch of a consultation to seek views on how best to operate the pupil premium:

> Schools should be engines of social mobility. They should provide the knowledge, and the tools, to enable talented young people to overcome accidents of birth and an inheritance of disadvantage in order to enjoy greater opportunities.

Sarah Teather, the Children's Minister, commented at the same consultation:

> For too long social background has been a deciding factor in a child's achievement and future prospects. In a fair society, it's the Government's responsibility to close the gulf in achievement, where the poorest children are almost three times less likely to leave school with five good General Certificates of Secondary Education (GCSEs) than their richer classmates.

The most disadvantaged pupils have a tendency to receive the worst teaching. A child on FSM has around three times worse odds of achieving good school outcomes, compared to a non-FSM child, at every point in their education. The greatest indicator of a child's achievement is the highest educational qualification of their mother.

## The principles of the pupil premium

The key principles of the pupil premium are to:

- break down a segregated education system;
- promote greater social mobility by broadening the opportunities for those from deprived backgrounds to go to university and have better employment prospects;
- encourage successful schools to admit poorer children by giving them a financial incentive;
- give greater freedom to schools, academies and Pupil Referral Units (PRUs) as to how they spend the pupil premium, by not ring-fencing the funding at school level;
- ensure a more consistent and common level of funding for the pupil premium, no matter where a child or young person lives in England;
- allocate an equal amount of money for the pupil premium, irrespective of whether the child is in the primary or secondary phase of education;
- make the criteria for the eligibility and the allocation of the pupil premium a less complex process.

## Those who benefit from the pupil premium

The children and young people identified by the coalition government as benefiting most from the pupil premium are those aged five to sixteen, within Reception to Year 11, who live in families with an annual income of less than £16,000 and who are:

- eligible for FSM in the last six years (known as the Deprivation Pupil Premium);
- looked after children (known as the Looked After Child Pupil Premium);
- children from an armed service family (known as the Service Child Pupil Premium).

## The amount of pupil premium allocated to disadvantaged children

In the financial year 1st April 2012 to the 31st March 2013:

- those eligible for FSM in the last six years receive £600;
- those who are looked after children (LAC) receive £600;
- those from armed service families receive £250.

Table 4.1 provides a useful at-a-glance chart of how much money schools can gain from the pupil premium, according to the number on roll on FSM.

*Table 4.1* Pupil premium funding at £600 per FSM pupil per year

| Percentage of free school meals | | | | | | |
|---|---|---|---|---|---|---|
| *No. on roll* | *10%* | *20%* | *30%* | *50%* | *70%* | *90%* |
| 50 | £3,000 | £6,000 | £9,000 | £15,000 | £21,000 | £27,000 |
| 100 | £6,000 | £12,000 | £18,000 | £30,000 | £42,000 | £54,000 |
| 250 | £15,000 | £30,000 | £45,000 | £75,000 | £105,000 | £135,000 |
| 500 | £30,000 | £60,000 | £90,000 | £150,000 | £210,000 | £270,000 |
| 750 | £45,000 | £90,000 | £135,000 | £225,000 | £315,000 | £405,000 |
| 1,000 | £60,000 | £120,000 | £180,000 | £300,000 | £420,000 | £540,000 |
| 2,000 | £120,000 | £240,000 | £360,000 | £600,000 | £840,000 | £1,080,000 |

In 2014–2015, the pupil premium is expected to rise to approximately £1,200 per FSM child and LAC. The pupil premium provides additional per pupil funding, on top of the existing funding for schools. Schools, academies and PRUs are free to spend the additional funding as they choose, providing it raises the achievement of eligible disadvantaged pupils.

## How to make effective use of the pupil premium

There is no blue print or 'one-size-fits-all' model being promoted by the government for using the pupil premium. The coalition government recommend three approaches for using the pupil premium. These are:

- one-to-one tuition for those pupils struggling to keep up in class;
- reduced class sizes;
- pastoral support, particularly for those pupils from armed service families.

Some headteachers, when consulted by the DfE in July 2012, offered the following suggestions for making best use of the pupil premium:

- hiring additional qualified and well-trained teachers;
- paying existing high-quality teachers more to work with the most complex and vulnerable pupils, particularly in schools in the most challenging areas;
- maximising the skills, knowledge and expertise by increasing the number of advanced skills teachers (ASTs) and excellent teachers, to teach pupil premium pupils and model good practice in working with these children, within and beyond the school;
- creating smaller classes to deliver a more personalised and tailored curriculum;
- funding additional extra-curricular activities, residential trips and after-school opportunities;
- extending the school day to increase the range of after-school activities;
- purchasing additional ICT and multi-media resources for targeted pupils;
- procuring additional good-quality learning support staff, e.g. learning mentors, higher level teaching assistants (HLTAs) with specific roles;
- establishing a nurture group in school;
- creating a 'Quiet Place' within the school which offers therapeutic interventions;
- enhancing the school's pastoral support system by offering counselling and personal tutors for targeted pupils;
- purchasing additional specialist support from external agencies, voluntary and community sectors, e.g. speech and language therapy, behaviour support;
- funding pupil-led action research to identify and inform best practice in using the additional funding;
- validating best practice in using the pupil premium by engaging in external moderation.

Teachers, when consulted on using the pupil premium, suggested in addition to the above:

- improving the classroom or school environment;
- extending curriculum breadth through music, art or physical education (PE);
- providing catch-up classes during term time for those falling behind.

Not every strategy offered by headteachers and teachers gives a good impact. For example:

- creating smaller classes does little to boost achievement when the targeted children are not being taught by good or outstanding teachers;
- one-to-one tuition is expensive and will only work if a good-quality professional is delivering the intervention;

- ability grouping may bring added stigma to the most disadvantaged underachieving pupils in the bottom group;
- recruiting extra teaching assistants will only work if they are confident in modelling and using meta-cognitive strategies in their support work;
- extending the school day to fit in after-school activities will not benefit those vulnerable or disadvantaged pupils who are tagged and on curfews to be home by 4pm.

The coalition government to date, at the time of writing this book, has not published any guidance for schools on how to use the pupil premium. However, in May 2011, the Sutton Trust published a *Toolkit of Strategies to Improve Learning*, which offered schools a summary on what to spend the pupil premium on. In July 2012, the Sutton Trust Education Endowment Foundation published *The Teaching and Learning Toolkit*, which provides updated guidance for teachers and schools on how to use their resources to improve the attainment of disadvantaged pupils. The toolkit suggests that different ways of using the pupil premium have different impacts on pupil attainment. It supports teachers in schools to make informed decisions, using evidence-based practice, as to which strategies give the greatest impact.

Table 4.2 provides an overview of the impact of different uses of the pupil premium.

The low impact of teaching assistants is likely to be due to teachers not utilising them specifically to improve targeted pupils' learning by having a pedagogical role, i.e. by delivering additional interventions.

The Sutton Trust identifies what really works in improving the attainment of disadvantaged pupils. This includes:

- teaching through the eyes of children;
- talking about learning, learning about learning and thinking about thinking;
- promoting active group and paired learning activities;
- encouraging pole bridging (where pupils articulate to others what they did to learn something or to solve a problem);
- using visual prompts and displays to promote learning;
- giving pupils brain breaks between learning activities;
- using thinking skills, mind mapping, open questioning and giving sufficient thinking time to pupils;
- providing pupils with opportunities to self-review their learning.

*Table 4.2* Pupil premium approaches and their effectiveness

| Approach | Potential gain | Cost | Applicability | Impact |
|---|---|---|---|---|
| *Feedback* – where information is given to the learner and/or teacher about the learners' performance relative to learning goals, with the aim of improving pupils' learning. | 9 months | ££ | Primary, Secondary, English, Maths, Science | Very high impact for a low cost |
| *Meta-cognition* – learning to learn where teaching approaches make learners think about learning more explicitly. | 8 months | ££ | Primary, Secondary, English, Maths, Science | High impact for a low cost |
| Peer tutoring | 6 months | ££ | Primary, Secondary, English, Maths, Science | High impact for a low cost |
| Early Years intervention | 6 months | £££££ | Primary, English, Maths | High impact for a very high cost |
| One-to-one | 5 months | £££££ | Primary, Secondary, English, Maths | Moderate impact for a very high cost |
| Homework | 5 months | £ | Primary, Secondary, English, Maths, Science | Moderate impact for a very low or no cost |
| ICT | 4 months | ££££ | Primary, Secondary, all subjects | Moderate impact for a high cost |
| Phonics | 4 months | £ | Primary, English | Moderate impact for a very low cost |
| Parental involvement | 3 months | £££ | Primary, Secondary, English, Maths, Science | Moderate impact for a moderate cost |
| Sports participation | 3 months | £££ | Primary, Secondary, English, Maths, Science | Moderate impact for a moderate cost |
| Summer schools | 3 months | £££ | Primary, Secondary, English, Maths | Moderate impact for a moderate cost |
| Reducing class sizes | 3 months | £££££ | Primary, Secondary, English, Maths | Moderate impact for a very high cost |
| After-school programmes | 2 months | ££££ | Primary, Secondary, English, Maths, Science | Low impact for a high cost |
| Individualised instruction | 2 months | ££ | Primary, Secondary, English, Maths, Science | Low impact for a low cost |
| Learning styles | 2 months | £ | Primary, Secondary, all subjects | Low impact for a very low or no cost |
| Arts participation | 1 month | ££ | Primary, Secondary, English, Maths, Science | Very low impact for a low cost |
| Performance pay | 0 months | £££ | Primary, Secondary, English, Maths, Science | Very low/no impact for a moderate cost |
| Teaching assistants | 0 months | ££££ | Primary, Secondary, English, Maths, Science | Very low/no impact for a high cost |
| Ability grouping | + or − 1 month | £ | Primary, Secondary, English, Maths, Science | Very low or negative impact for a very low or no cost |
| Block timetabling | + or − 1 month | £ | Primary, Secondary, English, Maths, Science | Very low or negative impact for a very low or no cost |
| Wearing school uniform | + or − 1 month | £ | Primary, Secondary, English, Maths, Science | Very low or negative impact for a very low or no cost |

(The Sutton Trust Education Endowment Foundation 2012: 2)

## Monitoring and evaluating the impact of the pupil premium

Schools are required to publish online on their website information about how they have used the pupil premium. This requirement makes it essential for schools, academies and PRUs to monitor and evaluate the use and impact of the pupil premium. The DfE first began to evaluate the pupil premium findings in September 2012. The DfE intends to provide details of which are the most effective interventions. Until the DfE publishes this information, schools, academies and PRUs should continue to use The Sutton Trust's *The Teaching and Learning Toolkit*, published in July 2012.

Monitoring is the ongoing process of checking progress against objectives set. It entails the systematic collection of targeted pupils' attainment data, which gives an indication of the progress and achievements made by pupil premium children as they experience additional interventions. The type of questions to ask in relation to monitoring the pupil premium via data collection and analysis include the following:

- What are the key sources of data required?
- What are the most appropriate data collection methods to use?
- Who will collect the pupil premium data?
- How often will the pupil premium data need to be collected?
- What are the cost implications of collecting the pupil premium data?
- Who will analyse the pupil premium data?
- Who will use the pupil premium data?
- Who will report on the pupil premium data?

Table 4.3 provides a template for recording and tracking targeted pupil premium children's attainment each term, matched against the types of additional interventions they have been offered.

Monitoring entails gathering the necessary quantitative data, which helps to inform decision-making and improve the added value being created by the pupil premium. Monitoring asks the questions: 'What are we doing?' and 'Are we doing what we agreed we would do?' Monitoring provides essential inputs for evaluation and therefore forms an integral part of the overall evaluation process. Qualitative data may also be collected on a regular basis from key stakeholders who are experiencing implementing the pupil premium (e.g. teachers, teaching assistants), as well as those benefiting from engaging in the additional interventions (pupils).

Evaluation is the systematic process and objective assessment of the pupil premium in terms of its implementation, effectiveness and impact on targeted pupils' outcomes. Evaluation also helps to identify strengths and weaknesses, in addition to judging how well things are going. Evaluation asks the following key questions: 'Are we doing the right thing?', 'Are we doing it right?', 'Are there better ways of achieving the results?', 'Is there a way of measuring our effectiveness?' and 'How do we know whether we are being successful?' Evaluation is considered to be the essential precursor to change. Evaluation helps to inform decision-making and future planning, as well as improving practice in the use and implementation of the pupil premium. A robust evaluation process is based on collecting a combination of qualitative and quantitative information.

Table 4.4 provides a generic monitoring and evaluation framework, which senior leaders and SENCOs may find helpful to use.

*Table 4.3* Pupil premium intervention tracking grid

| Pupil premium intervention | First year of progress | | | Second year of progress | | | Third year of progress | | |
|---|---|---|---|---|---|---|---|---|---|
| | Autumn term | Spring term | Summer term | Autumn term | Spring term | Summer term | Autumn term | Spring term | Summer term |
| | | | | | | | | | |
| | | | | | | | | | |
| | | | | | | | | | |
| | | | | | | | | | |
| | | | | | | | | | |
| | | | | | | | | | |
| | | | | | | | | | |
| | | | | | | | | | |
| | | | | | | | | | |

Pupil's name: _____

Class/form: _____

Date started: _____

*Table 4.4* Generic monitoring and evaluation framework for the pupil premium

*Types of evaluation*

| Formative assessments and research (concept and design) | Monitoring (monitoring inputs, processes and outputs; assessing service quality) | Evaluation (assessing outcome and impact) | Cost-effectiveness analysis (including sustainability issues) |
|---|---|---|---|

*Questions to be answered by different types of monitoring and evaluation approaches*

| | | | |
|---|---|---|---|
| • Is an intervention needed? <br> • Who needs the intervention? <br> • How should the intervention be carried out? | • To what extent are planned activities actually realised? <br> • How well are the services provided? | • What outcomes are observed? <br> • What do the outcomes mean? <br> • Does the pupil premium make a difference? | • Should pupil premium priorities be changed or expanded? <br> • To what extent should pupil premium resources be reallocated? |

In conclusion, monitoring and evaluation are:

- about results, i.e. whether the additional interventions procured from the use of the pupil premium funding have enhanced the learning of targeted pupils;
- participative processes, engaging relevant stakeholders at all levels in an education organisation;
- key for agreeing and regulating the roles and responsibilities of those involved with the pupil premium.

### Checklist for monitoring and evaluating the pupil premium

- There are clear plans and procedures in place for monitoring and evaluating the pupil premium.
- Everyone involved understands the monitoring and evaluation processes being used.
- Monitoring and evaluation processes are robust and systematically undertaken.
- A senior leader has overall responsibility for overseeing the monitoring and evaluation of the pupil premium in the educational setting.
- A set of agreed common objectives are used in the monitoring and evaluation process.
- Everyone is clear that the effectiveness and impact of the pupil premium are the key focus in the monitoring and evaluation process.
- An external 'critical friend' offers an objective impartial view.
- Relevant stakeholders contribute to the evaluation process.
- An agreed timescale and deadline for reporting back on the pupil premium exists.
- Reporting back on the impact of the pupil premium in an accessible format for different audiences.

## Validating best practice in the pupil premium

Schools, academies and PRUs may wish to seek external validation for their good practice in using the pupil premium to improve the attainment of those pupils eligible for this additional funding.

This can be done in a range of different educational settings, using a self-evaluation framework to enable the organisation to evaluate their pupil premium work against a series of good practice evidence descriptors. The six aspects on the self-evaluation framework include: leadership, management and coordination; closing the attainment gap; value for money; empowering pupil voice; sharing good practice; and impact.

The pupil premium validation process entails four main steps. These are illustrated in Figure 4.1.

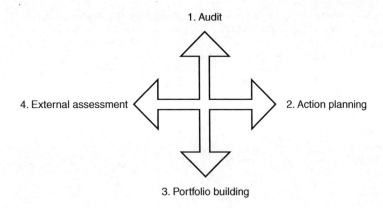

1. Audit

4. External assessment

2. Action planning

3. Portfolio building

*Figure 4.1* Pupil premium self-evaluation process

**Step 1: Undertaking the initial audit** using the self-evaluation review framework provided. Making 'best fit' judgements against the evidence descriptors for each of the six aspects, an educational setting will be able to assess their current position, as well as identify any gaps in pupil premium policy and provision to be improved.

**Step 2: Producing an action plan** which identifies the areas requiring further improvement, in relation to pupil premium policy and practice. These activities are then shared across a number of key staff, who each take responsibility for one of the six aspects. These staff form a pupil premium team, which is overseen by a senior leader.

**Step 3: Building a portfolio** to gather relevant evidence to meet all the evidence descriptors, for each of the six aspects. This evidence can be multi-media as well as documentary. The pupil premium team should meet on a regular basis to discuss and review the evidence being gathered. A completed portfolio of evidence record sheet for each of the six aspects should be included in the final portfolio, along with all the relevant evidence.

**Step 4: Going for the final validation** which entails an on-site evaluation and an off-site assessment of the portfolio, undertaken by another external leader. There is an expectation that the successful school, academy or PRU achieving a positive outcome will share their good practice with other schools locally.

Table 4.5 gives an example of one aspect of the pupil premium review framework. Table 4.6 provides an example of a portfolio of an evidence record sheet.

*Table 4.5* Pupil premium review framework for leadership, management and coordination

| Evidence descriptors | Emergent early stages ✓ or ✗ and date | Developing in progress ✓ or ✗ and date | Embedded fully in place ✓ or ✗ and date | Key source of evidence and evaluative comment |
|---|---|---|---|---|
| a  The leader of the setting has clarified with all key stakeholders who is eligible for the pupil premium, and how it could be utilised. | | | | |
| b  There is a member of the governing body or management board who is nominated for the pupil premium. | | | | |
| c  There is a designated member of the senior leadership team who has responsibility for strategically leading, managing and coordinating the pupil premium, across the setting. | | | | |
| d  There is a priority relating to the pupil premium on the educational setting's improvement plan. | | | | |
| e  Challenging and stretching pupil premium targets have been agreed, which indicate the high expectations for targeted pupils accessing this additional resource. | | | | |
| f  The leader of the setting builds capacity in the workforce to develop good and outstanding teaching and pastoral staff, to teach and support targeted pupils, e.g. ASTs, excellent teachers and TAs, an outstanding teacher programme and CPD for all staff. | | | | |
| g  The designated senior leader for the pupil premium reports each term to the governing body and the SLT on the use and effectiveness of the pupil premium. | | | | |

*Table 4.6* Portfolio of evidence record sheet for leadership, management and coordination

| Key evidence presented (two examples per descriptor) | Source of evidence | Examples of possible evidence |
|---|---|---|
| a<br>•<br>• | | PowerPoint presentation; minutes from key meetings; spreadsheet of list of eligible pupils |
| b<br>•<br>• | | Named governor in minutes of governors' meeting; outline of governor role for pupil premium |
| c<br>•<br>• | | Job description of senior leader for the pupil premium; any briefings and updates on pupil premium presented to SLT and governors |
| d<br>•<br>• | | School development plan extract; reports on progress towards meeting pupil premium priority on the development plan |
| e<br>•<br>• | | Examples of any individual pupil and whole school targets set for the pupil premium; example of individual pupil reports on progress made in meeting targets |
| f<br>•<br>• | | Staff CPD programme; staff evaluations from relevant training; in-house and external training delivered and accessed on pupil premium |
| g<br>•<br>• | | Two different reports on the use and effectiveness of the pupil premium delivered by the senior leader for the pupil premium |

Name of lead person collecting this evidence: _____

Job title/role: _____

Date evidence gathering commenced: _____

Date evidence collection completed: _____

Summative comments on the review and evidence gathering process for this aspect, e.g. what worked well; why it worked well; and what could be changed, improved or further developed:

Any other comment:

## Points to remember

- The pupil premium targets those pupils on FSM, or who are a looked after child or who are from an armed service family.
- The key aim of the pupil premium is to help close the attainment gap between poor disadvantaged pupils and their peers, who are more socially and economically advantaged.
- There is no blue-print or one-size-fits-all model for using the pupil premium.
- Monitoring is the systematic checking on progress and the gathering of information to establish the extent to which an initiative or programme is being implemented.
- Evaluation entails judging the quality, effectiveness, strengths and weaknesses of provision, based on robust evidence collected during review and monitoring processes.
- Value added is a measure that shows the difference a school makes to the educational outcomes of pupils, given their starting points.

## Further activities for reflection

1   How much value is the pupil premium adding in your organisation, in relation to closing the attainment gap for eligible SEND pupils?

2   What is working best in improving outcomes for those on the pupil premium in your organisation?

3   How is the pupil premium being monitored and evaluated in your setting?

4   How are the parents and carers of eligible SEND pupils being informed about how the pupil premium is benefiting their child?

5   What information is being published on the school website about the pupil premium and its use?

6   What evidence would you present to OFSTED to demonstrate the impact and effectiveness of the pupil premium?

# Chapter 5

# Meeting the **OFSTED** inspection requirements for **SEND**

**This chapter covers:**

- Key findings from the OFSTED HMI review of SEND
- Recommendations from the OFSTED HMI review of SEND
- OFSTED requirements for SEND and implications for the SENCO
- Making best use of the OFSTED *Subsidiary Guidance*
- Judging the effectiveness of additional provision
- Top tips for SENCOs preparing for the meeting with the OFSTED inspector
- OFSTED expectations of the SEND governor

## Key findings from the **OFSTED HMI** review of **SEND**

Her Majesty's Inspectors (HMI) with OFSTED undertook a review of SEND between April 2009 and March 2010 at the request of the government. The final report entitled *The Special Educational Needs and Disability Review: A Statement is not Enough* was published in September 2010. This review formed the coalition government's SEND Green Paper *Support and Aspiration: A New Approach to Special Educational Needs and Disability*.

The review of SEND by OFSTED focused on three aspects:

- assessment and identification;
- access to and quality of provision;
- evaluation and accountability.

Some of OFSTED's key findings from their SEND review report included:

- too much time was spent on assessing children to identify SEN, taking frontline workers away from early intervention and direct work with them;
- different services were found to use different assessments and to have different thresholds for securing additional support, making the process confusing;
- the term SEN was found to mean different things to different services;
- evaluation was found to be poor across services in relation to judging the quality and effectiveness of the additional support provided for pupils with SEN;
- there was a great variation in the number of pupils identified with SEND in schools; for example, anything from five per cent to seventy per cent out of a school's total pupil population, resulting in too many being identified at School Action, who just need better teaching and pastoral support;
- for all the money spent on SEN over the last seven years, SEN pupils' attainment and progress was still too low;

- pupils with SEN were found to be eight times more likely to be permanently excluded, compared to their peers;
- twenty-eight per cent of looked after children were found to have a statement of SEN;
- pupils with SEN were twice as likely to be eligible for FSM;
- there is no one model of provision that works best for SEN pupils.

Of all the key findings featured in the OFSTED SEND review report, the DfE commented on one in their SEND Green Paper:

> OFSTED report that the most important factor in determining the best outcomes for children with SEN is the quality of provision.
>
> (DfE 2011c: introduction, paragraph 33)

OFSTED concluded that good outcomes for SEND pupils are dependent on:

- good teaching and learning;
- close tracking and rigorous monitoring of progress;
- interventions put in place quickly and early;
- high expectations;
- promotion of independence.

In relation to when the best learning occurs among SEND pupils, OFSTED concluded this happened when teachers had:

- a detailed knowledge of the child;
- a thorough knowledge of appropriate teaching and learning strategies;
- good subject knowledge;
- a sound understanding of child development and how different learning difficulties and disabilities influence this.

## Recommendations from the OFSTED HMI review of SEND

OFSTED made many recommendations in their HMI review of SEND, and some of the most important are listed below.

- A school should analyse the effectiveness of generic teaching and support systems before deciding that a child has SEN.
- Local areas should consider using the same assessment system across all services.
- A child's access to additional services should not always depend on a formal process of assessment or medical diagnosis.
- Specific rights to additional provision, enshrined in law, should apply only to disabled children and young people where the Disability Discrimination Act, superseded by the Equality Act 2010, applies.
- Evaluation should focus on outcomes for children with additional needs.
- Good evaluation requires a system that tracks SEND pupils' progress securely and uses information rigorously and regularly to evaluate the impact of additional interventions.
- Schools, colleges and services should improve the quality of their evaluation of additional provision.
- All schools and services involved in any common assessment process should be held to account legally for SEND pupils' outcomes.
- The SEN Code of Practice and its statutory basis should be reviewed.
- Any further changes to SEND legislation or guidance should simplify current arrangements and improve consistency across different services.

For those readers who wish to view the full list of recommendations, these can be found on pages 13 and 14 of the OFSTED SEND review report published in September 2010.

## OFSTED requirements for SEND and implications for the SENCO

The final revised OFSTED inspection framework became effective from September 2012. The DfE in their White Paper entitled *The Importance of Teaching* commented:

> The new inspection framework will help to make sure that there is a better focus on the needs of all pupils, including the needs of pupils with Special Educational Needs and/or disabilities.
>
> (DfE 2010b: 6.18)

Similarly, in the DfE SEND Green Paper, it stated:

> We want a stronger focus by OFSTED on how well the education provided for disabled children and those with SEN meets their needs so that schools are properly held to account for both the outcomes and experiences of those children.
>
> (DfE 2011c: 3.77)

The school inspection framework focuses on four key areas. These are:

1   achievement of pupils at the school;
2   quality of teaching in the school;
3   the behaviour and safety of pupils at the school;
4   quality of leadership in, and management of, the school.

Overall, in relation to SEND, OFSTED inspectors will check:

- the school's aspirations for SEND pupils;
- SEND pupils' motivation;
- the extent to which SEND pupils use their initiative;
- whether SEND pupils have enough opportunities to work independently in lessons;
- whether SEND pupils have sufficient opportunities to learn collaboratively, with other peers;
- how well the education provided for SEND pupils meets their needs, particularly in relation to the outcomes and experiences for those pupils.

OFSTED will not use IEPs as the sole or main source of evidence of SEND pupils' progress, in view of IEP targets being variable in quality and lacking sufficient challenge.

Table 5.1 provides a useful at-a-glance guide to OFSTED's inspection of SEND.

Table 5.1 OFSTED SEND requirements with implications for the SENCO

| OFSTED INSPECTION AREA | OFSTED SEND REQUIREMENTS | IMPLICATIONS FOR THE SENCO |
|---|---|---|
| 1 Achievement of pupils at the school | How good the value added progress is for individual SEND pupils, based on their starting point on entry to the school and their age. | The SENCO has a robust moderation system in place for all teacher assessment of SEND pupils' progress. |
| | How clear the difference is between SEND pupils who have barriers to learning and those pupils who are just simply underachieving (e.g. the correct identification of SEND pupils). | Moderation shows evidence of working with other schools/partners. |
| | Three-year attainment trends for SEND: expected rates of progress from Key Stage (KS)1 to KS2 (two levels of progress) and KS2 to KS4 (three levels of progress). | The progress datasets are used from the government's *Progression Guidance*, to judge how good SEND pupils' progress is. |
| | No comparison between the different types of SEND pupils will be made in a school, because the definitions are so variable, making comparison unreliable. | The SENCO can justify why some SEND pupils make above-average progress, and why others have performed below age-related expectations. |
| | | The SENCO collects SEND pupils' well-being data, which demonstrates progress in aspects such as attendance, exclusions, behaviour, self-esteem, independence. |
| 2 Quality of teaching in the school | How well lessons observed are well-planned to offer enough good-quality learning opportunities for SEND pupils. | The SENCO has evidence to demonstrate their impact on improving teachers' practice in teaching a diversity of SEND pupils, across the school. |
| | The extent to which teachers secure high-quality learning for SEND pupils by setting challenging tasks matched to pupils' specific learning needs. | The SENCO has evidence to show how far teachers across the school take on responsibility for SEND pupils in their classes. |
| | The quality of teaching and learning support provided for pupils with a range of SEND, aptitude and needs, to improve their learning. | Evidence from SENCO lesson observations across the school shows how teachers are using assessment information to set high expectations for SEND pupils. |
| | How effectively teachers use support staff in relation to the planning for their deployment; their briefing; how much time the teacher spends working with SEND pupils across the ability range; and how well small group interventions are taught. | The SENCO has evidence of how they evaluate teachers' monitoring and tracking data relating to SEND pupils' learning, in order to support curriculum differentiation and make any changes quickly and promptly. |

*Table 5.1 continued*

| OFSTED INSPECTION AREA | OFSTED SEND REQUIREMENTS | IMPLICATIONS FOR THE SENCO |
|---|---|---|
| 3  The behaviour and safety of pupils at the school | How many SEND pupils are poor attendees at school, have poor punctuality, experience fixed term and permanent exclusions or internal school exclusions/sent to a withdrawal room, and how many experience or are involved in bullying incidents. | The SENCO has evidence of how the behaviour of SEND pupils is tracked and monitored across the school. |
| | How rigorous the tracking of the behaviour and progress of those pupils who have identified behavioural difficulties is, and whether there is robust evidence of improvement in their behaviour and in their attitude to learning. | The SENCO can show evidence of SEND pupil 'voice' in relation to them having a say about their learning, safety and additional provision, e.g. from annual reviews or case studies. |
| | What the SEND pupils' views are in relation to their attitude to learning, their safety in school, particularly in relation to bullying. | Where appropriate, the SENCO can provide details about the composition of lower sets or teaching groups, e.g. how many SEND pupils are in these groups, how often they experience disruption to their learning because of poor behaviour of other peers in the same set or group, and the action taken to address this issue. |
| | How far SEND pupils' learning is disrupted in lessons across the school. | The SENCO has evidence of 'reasonable adjustments' being made to ensure the inclusion of BESD and autistic spectrum disorder (ASD) pupils in school. |
| 4  Quality of leadership in, and management of, the school | How accurate the identification of pupils who have SEND is in the school. Whether leaders and managers, including the SENCO, have considered thoroughly the quality of teaching and support as part of the identification of SEND pupils. How effectively the school evaluates the quality of teaching for pupils with SEND, and improves it where necessary. | The SENCO has evidence of how they effectively lead SEND whole school, to effect change and improvement. |
| | How thorough the school's evaluation is of the progress made by individual SEND pupils, based on age and prior attainment. | The SENCO has evidence of how he/she contributes to whole school self-evaluation, in relation to SEND. |
| | How rigorous the school's arrangements are to moderate assessment of attainment for low-attaining pupils, including those with SEND. | The SENCO can provide evidence to show the effectiveness of the SEND governor in providing challenge and acting as a 'critical friend' for SEND. This may be in the form of reports to the governing body and minutes from SENCO meetings with the SEND governor, which take place at least once each term. |
| | How far additional interventions for SEND pupils show that they have made accelerated progress. | |
| | How the school's analysis of additional intervention data has been compared to the national datasets for pupils performing below age-expected levels, in order to judge whether progress is good enough. | |
| | The quality of the school's provision map. | |
| | How thoroughly the SEND governor is aware of the accuracy of the identification of pupils with SEND; the quality of their progress; and the effectiveness of the additional interventions, including the use of the pupil premium, in meeting these pupils' needs. | |

## Making best use of the OFSTED *Subsidiary Guidance*

In January 2012, OFSTED published *Subsidiary Guidance*, which was later updated in March 2012 and September 2012. This document contains specific information relating to pupils with SEND. There are two parts to the guidance. Part One focuses on providing more in-depth information for inspectors on each of the four areas in the new inspection framework. Part two covers further guidance for specific settings such as PRUs, special schools, mainstream schools with specially resourced provision for SEND pupils and alternative off-site provision. It is important for SENCOs to read this *Subsidiary Guidance* carefully, when preparing evidence for inspectors.

Pages 12 to 14 in Part One of the *Subsidiary Guidance* relates to the achievement of pupils with special educational needs. The key points from this section include:

- Inspectors must not assume that levels of attainment in special schools will be below those expected of pupils of a similar age nationally.
- A category of special educational need, e.g. ASD, does not give an indication of the level a pupil with this SEN would be working at, given their starting point on entry to a school. For example, one pupil may be working towards A* GCSE grades and another pupil of the same age with ASD may be working towards Level P6.
- Inspectors need to take into account the proportion of pupils in a school with SEN that are related to cognitive difficulties. For example, where SLD or MLD pupils make up a large proportion of pupils in a small inclusive primary school or a large resource base for SLD in a standard-sized primary school, then inspectors should only consider the attainment of those pupils without particular cognitive difficulties.
- Inspectors need to evaluate the progress made by SEN pupils in a school by using the national data on progress made by low-attaining pupils, and comparing this with the school's own rigorous analysis of progress. There is not an expectation that all of these SEN pupils will make two levels of progress from KS1 to KS2, or three levels of progress from KS2 to KS4.
- When inspectors evaluate SEN pupils' achievement, they should note if pupils who receive additional interventions are demonstrating accelerated or sustained progress.
- Inspectors should also evaluate the school's arrangements for ensuring the accuracy of its SEN pupil performance data, e.g. the rigorous moderation within a school and across a local authority/locality to ensure the accuracy and validity of P level (teacher assessment) data.
- Inspectors also need to look at patterns (trends) in the performance of different groups of SEN pupils over time in a school or academy.
- Inspectors should use the datasets 2–3 of the *Progression Guidance* 2010–2011 as a guide to provide challenge when judging SEN pupils' progress in a school or academy. School leaders are expected to be using these datasets as a first level of analysis of SEN pupils' progress within the educational setting.
- Inspectors will judge the value added (VA) progress made by SEN pupils, including those on P levels, by analysing the average point score conversion data, and the charts in RAISEonline for English and Mathematics.
- In view of IEPs not being a statutory requirement and the targets on them not being moderated, inspectors are unlikely to use these when judging SEN pupils' achievement.
- Inspectors should consider carefully the extent to which success in qualifications and awards demonstrates that SEN pupils have made progress in their skills, knowledge or understanding, in view of curriculum changes.
- Inspectors are likely to tack a sample of SEN pupils to assess their experience of a school day or part of a school day, in order to judge the experience, progress and learning of these pupils in the context with other pupils' experiences.
- Inspectors will explore how the school supports its most behaviourally challenging pupils, in order to check out the school's ethos and approach to equality and diversity, e.g. those with BESD and ASD, to ensure reasonable adjustments have been made to help them to be included in school.

In mainstream schools with specially resourced provision for SEN pupils, inspectors will:

- observe classes involving SEN pupils from the resourced provision;
- see how far teachers plan thoroughly for the deployment of specialist support staff, in particular how they brief them on what the SEN pupils are expected to learn and clarify the teaching assistant's role or learning support activity;
- look at how teachers make full use of agreed specialist approaches, advice or equipment, in helping to remove SEN pupils' barriers to learning;
- analyse the achievements of resourced provision pupils, and explore and identify the reasons for any difference between the achievement of these pupils compared to those SEN pupils in the mainstream classes;
- explore with the teacher in charge of the resourced provision how well the SEN pupils are achieving in comparison to those SEN pupils in the mainstream, the quality of the resourced provision, and how their leadership and management contributes to these pupils' outcomes.

When a SEN pupil is accessing alternative/off-site provision, inspectors will consider:

- how well the school identifies appropriate alternative provision and matches it to the SEN pupils' needs and interests;
- how the school has assessed the quality and safety of the provision;
- the quality of the information provided by the school to the off-site provider about the pupil's SEN, behaviour and literacy levels;
- how the school monitors and evaluates the SEN pupils' attendance, behaviour and progress at the alternative/off-site provision;
- the quality of pastoral support given to SEN pupils attending provision off-site.

Where the SENCO is overseeing additional interventions for SEN pupils in developing their reading skills, it is important that they take note of the key aspects of reading and literacy that inspectors will consider during inspection. These transferable skills include:

- pupils' phonic decoding strategies and their knowledge of phonically irregular words;
- literal and inferential comprehension;
- higher-order reading skills, e.g. inference, appreciation of an author's style and awareness of themes;
- knowledge of books and authors, including similarities and differences between texts;
- attitudes and enjoyment;
- pupils' awareness of their own progress and development as a reader;
- support from school and home;
- teaching of reading, expectations and the school's reading culture.

## Judging the effectiveness of additional provision

Judging the effectiveness of additional provision, including teaching assistants, is a key role for the SENCO. The SENCO needs to take into account the expectation that SEN pupils receiving additional interventions such as a specific reading programme should make, on average, at least twice the normal rate of progress.

The aim of any additional intervention is to:

- remove barriers to learning;
- maximise progress;
- close the attainment gap;
- apply learning from the additional intervention across the curriculum.

When evaluating any additional intervention as part of SEN provision, the SENCO will find it useful to answer the following questions:

- Which additional interventions have had a direct impact on improving SEN pupils' learning?
- How have the additional interventions helped to improve SEN pupils' standards of work?
- Of all the additional interventions put in place for SEN pupils, which one has had the greatest impact and why?
- Which additional interventions or different SEN provision have not been effective, and what will you replace them with?

According to OFSTED:

> Good evaluation requires systems that track progress securely towards planned outcomes and information that is used rigorously and regularly to evaluate the impact of interventions.
>
> (OFSTED 2010: 14)

Teaching assistants, as an additional resource contributing to SEN provision, require the SENCO to evaluate the impact of their work on SEN pupils' learning. The government's SEND Green Paper commented on teaching assistants:

> For teaching assistants to have a positive impact they need to be trained, supported, deployed and managed effectively.
>
> (DfE 2011c: 3.27)

In the subsequent DfE SEND White Paper, it was stated in next steps:

> We will be awarding, from August 2012 ... the first round of the SEN Support Scholarship for talented support staff to gain degree-level qualifications to improve their knowledge and expertise.
>
> (DfE 2012: 3.15)

The following checklist will be useful for SENCOs who are evaluating the effectiveness and impact of teaching assistant support. All teaching assistants should:

- be clear about what the SEN pupils they are supporting are expected to learn in the lesson;
- build on the SEN pupils' prior learning;
- enable the SEN pupils to work independently;
- check and review the SEN pupils' learning at the end of the lesson;
- model good learning approaches;
- show evidence of the impact of their support for learning, through improved SEN pupil outcomes.

## Top tips for SENCOs preparing for the meeting with the OFSTED inspector

The latest inspection process, with its focus on SEN pupils, is likely to engage the SENCO far more than under the previous school inspection regime. The following top tips offer the SENCO some practical guidance in preparing SEN evidence for the OFSTED inspector.

- **Build a SEN portfolio of evidence, which is kept updated**, and includes:
    - SEN staff team structure, giving length of service and SEN qualifications of staff, including who is the SEN governor;
    - SEN policy, with evidence of its last review;
    - SEN development plan;

- SEN register, showing numbers of SEN pupils moving up and down the SEN thresholds, and also coming off the register;
- record of SEN INSET delivered in school, with evidence of impact from staff;
- SEN data showing number of SEN pupils by gender and type of SEN;
- SEN pupil level attainment data on spreadsheet, showing three-year trends, also depicted pictorially using bar charts, line graphs depicting progress by cohort, year group and at individual pupil level;
- contextual information to accompany the SEN pupil-level attainment data, e.g. pupil attendance record, exclusion, FSM, LAC, summer birthday, one-parent family, etc.;
- minutes of meetings with the SEN governor, and examples of any recent SEN reports to governors;
- testimonials of the effectiveness of the SENCO and SEN provision from parents and carers, professionals from external agencies, and staff from other schools;
- evidence of the impact of the SENCO delivering school-to-school support in the role of a specialist leader of education;
- examples of any SEN publications or seminars and training the SENCO has delivered and attended outside school.

- **Give evidence of the evaluation of any new SEN intervention or recent SEN development** that the SENCO has introduced in the school, which may include evidence-based practice and small-scale action research.
- **Produce pupil case studies**, which show the diversity of SEN, and give supporting evidence on the nature of learning difficulty, the strategies and additional interventions put in place, with the impact on the pupils' outcomes. These need only be one side of A4 paper in length.
- **Produce a couple of staff case studies**, which illustrate how, as the SENCO, you have improved the classroom practice of another teacher, via coaching, mentoring and demonstration lessons, to enable them to meet the needs of a SEN pupil.
- **Give evidence of whole school SEN monitoring**, e.g. classroom walkthroughs, lesson observations, scrutiny of SEN pupils' work across the curriculum, staff and SEN pupil discussions.
- **Show evidence of familiarity with the relevant datasets in the *Progression Guidance***, and how you have used these to make comparative judgements about SEN pupils' progress in your school.
- **Provide evidence of moderation of teacher assessment, P-level assessment**, which has taken place in school, and also beyond, in a local cluster, to help validate judgements about pupil progress and attainment.

The SENCO may find it useful to refer to the OFSTED inspector's document entitled *Special Educational Needs and/or Disabilities in Mainstream Schools: A Briefing Paper for Section 5 Inspectors* (2011), alongside OFSTED's September 2012 *Subsidiary Guidance*.

### Sample questions an OFSTED inspector may ask the SENCO

It is essential that the SENCO always makes three copies of all the above information. One copy is for the OFSTED inspector, the second copy is for the headteacher and the third copy is for the SENCO, who should bring this information with them to the meeting with the OFSTED inspector.

The following questions are examples of the type of questions an OFSTED inspector may ask the SENCO.

1    Achievement of SEND pupils

- How are you using the RAISEonline data to inform target setting for SEND pupils?
- Which cohort of SEND pupils are underachieving, and what is being done to address the issue?
- During the last twelve months, how many SEND pupils came off the SEND register?
- How are SEND pupils being involved in reviewing their learning and progress, across the curriculum?

2   Quality of teaching

- How have you supported class/subject teachers in effectively deploying teaching assistants?
- How do you ensure the skills SEND pupils learn in their additional intervention sessions are consistently being transferred across the curriculum?
- What action have you taken to address any poor-quality teaching of SEND pupils?

3   The behaviour and safety of SEND pupils

- How do you monitor and track the behaviour and attendance of SEND pupils?
- Where the behaviour of a SEND pupil is causing concern, how do you address this?
- How do you know SEND pupils feel safe and free from bullying in this school?

4   Quality of leadership in and management of SEND

- How are you engaging the 'harder-to-reach' parents of SEND pupils?
- How are you evaluating the effectiveness of partnership working with parents, external agencies and other schools in removing barriers to SEND pupils' learning?
- How is the SEND governor engaged in monitoring SEND policy and provision?

## OFSTED expectations of the SEND governor

Governance is given greater focus in the revised OFSTED inspection framework, and will feature as one paragraph in the final school inspection report, following inspection. Inspectors will be interested in the effectiveness of the SEND governor. They will check this through governing body minutes, discussions with the headteacher, the SENCO, parents and pupils.

OFSTED inspectors will expect the SEND governor to have:

- a clear understanding and knowledge about their role and duties in ensuring the school meets SEND statutory requirements, including equalities legislation;
- an awareness of the school's strengths and weaknesses in SEND, giving an indication as to how they know these;
- an awareness of the main SEND issues the school is facing, and how well the headteacher and SENCO are tackling the improvement in SEND;
- an awareness of the views and concerns of SEND pupils and their parents, responding to these appropriately, as an objective 'critical friend';
- been actively involved in monitoring, evaluating and reviewing the effectiveness of the school's SEND policy and the SEND development plan;
- the confidence to ask the headteacher and the SENCO challenging questions, with regard to improving the quality of teaching and the additional provision for SEND pupils;
- knowledge of the range of partnerships the school engages in, to improve outcomes for SEND pupils, and how effective each is;
- undertaken relevant ongoing training in SEND, and can comment on the impact of this in supporting them in their role;
- confidence in disseminating their SEND knowledge gained from training and discussion with the SENCO to the other members on the school's governing body.

### Exemplar OFSTED inspection questions for SEND governors, with answers

The following questions are examples of what an OFSTED inspector may ask the SEND governor, as part of the on-site inspection evidence trail. The suggested responses to each question provide a model for SEND governors to base their own answers on.

Q1  What are the strengths and weaknesses of SEND in the school and how do you know?

A1  The SEND governor would refer to the SEND pupil-level attainment and well-being data; the annual report to the governing body; and feedback from SEND pupils, their parents and carers, and from the staff, including discussions with the SENCO.

Q2  What have been the main barriers to learning for SEND pupils and how has the school overcome them?

A2  A good response to this question would entail the SEND governor talking about their own involvement in the monitoring and evaluation of SEND. For example, undertaking joint paired classroom walkthroughs with the SENCO, and having a focused discussion with the SENCO each term on SEND pupil progress in relation to their learning, curriculum access, behaviour and attendance.

Q3  What has been done to improve and further develop productive partnership working with parents of SEND pupils?

A3  The SEND governor would mention their attendance at governor drop-in sessions and informal parent coffee mornings, held at school, where they clarify their role as 'a champion for parents and families', and also bring any issues back to the SENCO and the senior leadership team, in relation to how the school could further improve their partnership working with parents of SEND pupils. It would be good practice if the governor could quote a couple of brief case studies of how they have helped to improve a SEND pupil's parents engagement with the school.

Q4  What is the governor's view on the quality of leadership of SEND in the school?

A4  The SEND governor would relate how the SENCO has helped teachers across the school, to differentiate the curriculum appropriately, by delivering a whole school INSET on the topic and offering drop-in sessions on differentiation each term. The SEND governor may also relate how the SENCO has reviewed the role of teaching assistants, and allocated SEND aspects to each, to develop their professional skills and knowledge, and improve the effectiveness of their support for learning.

Q5  What is the governor's view on how funding and resources for SEND pupils are used in the school?

A5  A good response from the SEND governor to this question would include a mention of how they see the school's provision map each term, and receive a budget breakdown twice a year on SEND income and expenditure. This also indicates which SEND pupils are eligible for pupil premium funding, how this is being used and what has been the impact of additional funding on SEND pupils' outcomes. The SEND governor may also mention how the SENCO and School Business Manager have used the SEN/Additional Educational Needs (AEN) Best Value Toolkit to evaluate good value for money in SEND expenditure, in terms of outcomes for SEND pupils.

---

**Points to remember**

- The most important factor in determining the best outcomes for SEN pupils is the quality of provision.
- Evaluation should focus on the outcomes for SEN pupils.
- IEPs will not be used as the sole or main source of evidence of SEN pupils' progress in OFSTED school inspections.
- SEN pupils receiving additional interventions should demonstrate accelerated or sustained progress at the end of the programme.
- School leaders and SENCOs should be using the *Progression Guidance* 2010–2011 datasets 2–3 to support the analysis of SEN pupils' progress.
- OFSTED inspectors will be exploring the effectiveness of the SEND governor.

## Further activities for reflection

1    In your role as an SLE supporting a newly appointed SENCO in another school, what advice would you give them in readiness for an OFSTED inspection?

2    What will you include in your SENCO report to governors on the impact and outcomes of all the additional interventions being delivered to SEN pupils in the school?

3    As SENCO, how would you make best use of OFSTED's *Subsidiary Guidance*, with teachers and teaching assistants, at a whole school INSET on meeting the needs of SEN pupils?

4    How will you as SENCO monitor the effectiveness of teaching assistants across the school, and use the findings to deploy these supporting adults more effectively?

5    After reading OFSTED's 2010 report on the review of SEND, what three improvements in SEN are top priorities in your school, academy or PRU?

6    What is the analysis of your school's SEN pupils' progress telling you, when compared with the *Progression Guidance* 2010–2011 datasets, for your particular key stage?

# Chapter 6

# Quality assuring school-to-school support for SEN

**This chapter covers:**

- The concept, principles and purpose of quality assurance
- Quality assurance indicators for school-to-school support in SEN
- Introduction to the school-to-school improvement self-review process
- The school-to-school improvement self-review aspects and stages
- Cameo of best practice of SENCO engagement in the award process

## The concept of quality assurance

Quality assurance (QA) is the process of systematically monitoring different aspects of a service, a policy, an initiative or new programme to check that it is 'fit for purpose', meets expectations and quality standards, and leads to a positive outcome for pupils. Quality assurance refers to the attitudes, actions and procedures that, together with quality control activities, ensure that standards are maintained and enhanced.

An effective quality assurance system must have agreement on its purpose and methods for collecting relevant evidence. The QA system should also include a feedback process to keep stakeholders informed about the progress made in improving the quality of educational provision and outcomes for pupils.

## Ten principles of quality assurance

1. Quality assurance principles, purpose and expectations are set out clearly in a robust QA policy, for all the school or academy workforce to understand and follow.
2. It is everyone's responsibility in the school or academy to contribute to ensuring quality outcomes for all pupils.
3. A culture and ethos of excellence exists in the school or academy, which encourages staff to be innovative in order to increase the quality, efficiency and effectiveness of their work.
4. Training and professional development for QA is provided to staff involved in the process.
5. Quality assurance decision-making is based on accurate information, which is made available to staff, when they need it.
6. Constructive professional dialogue on continuous improvement is encouraged among the staff.
7. The work of teachers and non-teaching staff is monitored and evaluated against the relevant national professional standards, as part of the quality assurance process.
8. Management at all levels in the school or academy continually assess their effectiveness in ensuring staff understand and follow the quality assurance mission policy and expectations.
9. Key stakeholders within and beyond the school or academy receive QA reports to keep them informed about improvement.
10. Good practice in quality assurance is disseminated to other schools and academies.

## The purpose of quality assurance

Quality assurance serves several purposes in a school or academy. The key ones are to:

- improve the monitoring and evaluation system and process;
- inform potential future staff, parents and pupils about the quality and effectiveness of the educational provision on offer;
- teach learners who move through the school or academy about the positive values of excellence in striving to meet their personal best;
- encourage the school or academy to continually reflect on their work, in order to inform transformational change.

QA entails reflecting on the school's or academy's practices in order to redefine goals, reposition the school or academy, and review strategies to attain existing goals. The following questions may be of value to the SENCO, to enable them to reflect on their school-to-school improvement work in SEN.

- What are you trying to do and why are you trying to do it?
- How are you trying to effect SEN improvement in another school?
- Why are you trying to effect SEN improvement in the way you have chosen?
- Why do you consider the improvement approach you are using is the best way?
- What evidence have you collected which shows the impact of your school-to-school improvement work in SEN?

## Quality assurance indicators for school-to-school support in SEN

A SENCO who is providing school-to-school improvement support for SEN in another school will be expected to evidence the impact of their work. Table 6.1 offers some quality assurance key indicators, with the type of evidence a SENCO could gather for each.

*Table 6.1* Quality assurance indicators for SEN with evidence

| INDICATORS | EVIDENCE |
| --- | --- |
| Improved progress of SEN pupils in specific curriculum subjects | Validated subject pupil-level attainment data |
| Improved SEN pupils' school attendance | Pupil-level school attendance data |
| Improved SEN pupils' behaviour | Behaviour incident log, pupil attitude to self and school (PASS) data, rewards and sanctions record, exclusions data |
| Greater progress made by individual SEN pupils who were underachieving | Five- and three-year trend tracking and attainment data |
| Improved quality of teaching and learning for SEN pupils | Lesson observations, classroom walkthroughs, discussion with pupils and teachers, work scrutiny |
| Improved teacher attitudes towards the inclusion of SEN pupils in mainstream lessons | Lesson observations, teacher interviews, pupil interviews, attitude surveys |
| Improved staff professional development in SEN | Staff evaluations on the impact of training to their classroom practice, classroom walkthroughs, focused lesson observations, discussion with pupils |
| Improved use of AfL, data analysis and tracking of SEN pupils' progress | Scrutiny of teachers tracking data, sampling of teacher planning, moderation of SEN pupils' work by teachers |
| Improved examination and test results for SEN pupils | School internal and external examination results |
| Improved learning support and pastoral care for SEN pupils | Snapshot lesson observations, observations of TAs delivering intervention groups, discussion with the pastoral leaders and sampling of SEN pupils' pastoral records |
| Improved parental views about the school's SEN provision | Discussion with SEN pupils' parents, evidence from parents' comments on their child's annual review, discussion with the SEN governor, and fewer or no parental complaints about SEN provision being recorded |

A SENCO providing school-to-school support for SEN should reflect upon their work in relation to quality and effectiveness, against each of the school improvement aspects, in the school improvement cycle. Figure 6.1 illustrates this cycle.

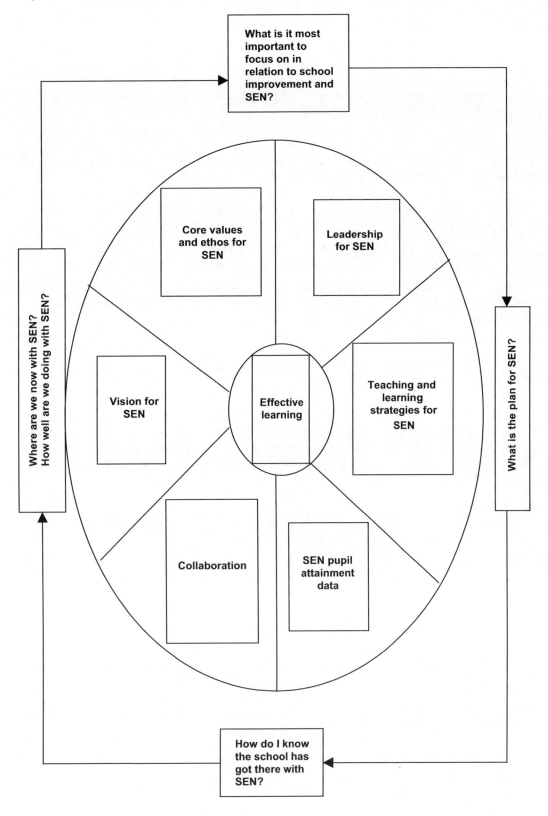

*Figure 6.1* The school improvement cycle for quality assuring SEN

## Introduction to the school-to-school improvement self-review process

At the time of writing this book, the NCSL were in the process of developing a quality assurance framework for evaluating the effectiveness and impact of teaching schools. Until the time such a framework is published by the NCSL, I, as author of this book, have produced a streamlined generic self-review framework, for evaluating and quality assuring a chosen area of school-to-school improvement support. The self-review framework has been piloted by a teaching school in Tameside during 2011–2012.

Outstanding teaching schools may be interested in engaging with the School-to-School Improvement Partnership self-review process. The process offers external validation via moderation, to successful educational settings who meet and fulfil the external assessment requirements.

The School-to-School Improvement Partnership self-review process is grounded in evidence-based practice, and entails the following stages:

1   undertaking the initial audit;
2   producing an action plan;
3   building a portfolio of evidence;
4   final external validation.

The outstanding educational setting, who is supporting another school, chooses one area of school improvement partnership working, e.g. SEND, or any other area which fits in with the OFSTED inspection schedule, or the DfE areas of work, for the specialist leader of education.

The School-to-School Improvement Partnership self-review process meets the DfE, OFSTED and the NCSL expectations and requirements in relation to delivering effective school-to-school support for improvement. Figure 6.2 illustrates the four stages of the quality assurance (self-review) process, while offering some reflective questions for further consideration.

While there is no set timescale for completing the self-review process, as this is governed by the context in which the teaching school or SLE is working in partnership with the other school, the majority of educational settings prefer a timeframe of between twelve to eighteen months for judging impact. Upon a successful final quality assurance outcome, the lead school, academy or PRU may choose a different area of school-to-school improvement partnership work for the next self-review journey.

**1. Baseline current position –
how are we doing?**
- Where are we now with this **one** area of school-to-school improvement work?
- What evidence have we already got of our current position on this one area of school improvement work?

**4. Reviewing and assessing progress**
- What actions need to be taken next if we still have some aspects of partnership working to be addressed in the area for improvement?
- What are our strengths in relation to this one area?
- How do we know we have achieved the expected outcomes in the school improvement area of school-to-school support?
- Are we ready to go forward for the final external validation?
- Next steps, following the assessment judgement?

**2. Action planning – what more should we do?**
- How can we further improve our partnership working in this area?
- What targets should be set?
- What action do we need to take to move policy and practice forward?
- Who will do what actions?
- What is a realistic timescale to meet the priorities and activities set?
- What resources will be required?
- What are the success criteria?
- What outcomes do we want?

**3. Evidence gathering and monitoring progress**
- What evidence will be gathered to demonstrate success and good practice in school-to-school support in the one area of school improvement?
- Are there any aspects of school-to-school partnership working that are problematic in gathering the required evidence?
- Are agreed actions happening?
- Is the partnership working team keeping on track with tasks set?
- Are the outcomes from ongoing monitoring being recorded systematically and electronically?

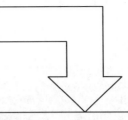
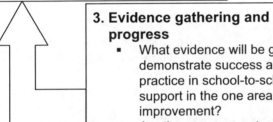
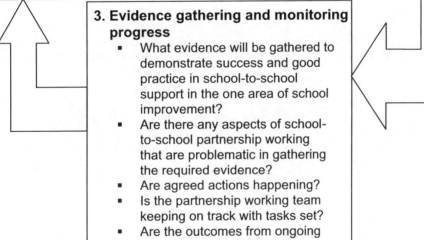

*Figure 6.2* Stages in the school-to-school improvement self-review process

### *The benefits of engaging in the School-to-School Improvement Partnership self-review process*

Engagement in the School-to-School Improvement Partnership self-review process brings several benefits. For example, it offers participating educational settings:

- a robust evidence-based process that meets internal and external accountability requirements;
- a manageable, streamlined cost-effective quality assurance process;
- the opportunity for relevant staff to engage in a process that enhances their professional development;
- a self-review and quality assurance process that impacts positively on pupil outcomes;
- the opportunity to gain external recognition and validation for best practice in school-to-school support, within or across a local cluster group.

## The school-to-school improvement self-review aspects and stages

The generic school-to-school improvement self-review framework provides a valuable quality assurance tool to audit current school-to-school support and identify strengths and gaps where further development is required in the chosen area, e.g. SEND.

### *1 Undertaking the initial audit*

It is best practice if the self-review audit is undertaken by the headteacher and the senior member of staff who is going to strategically oversee the work taking place in the partner school where improvement is required.

There are six key aspects on the generic school-to-school improvement partnership framework (audit). These cover:

1  strategic leadership;
2  professional development;
3  stakeholder involvement;
4  partnership working;
5  quality assurance;
6  disseminating good practice.

All of the six aspects on the school-to-school improvement partnership working audit each have five good practice evidence descriptors, by which 'best fit' judgements can be made in relation to the chosen area of school-to-school support for improvement. There are three columns on the audit to tick, which reflect the current position. These are emergent, developing and embedded.

Table 6.2 illustrates the full self-review framework for audit use. Table 6.3 offers a template for the action plan.

*Table 6.2* School-to-school improvement partnership working self-review audit
(For use when reviewing ONE area of school improvement work)

1  Strategic leadership

| Good practice evidence descriptors | Emergent ✓ (Early stages at 30%) | Developing ✓ (Work in progress at 50%) | Embedded ✓ (Fully in place at 100%) | Evidence and impact |
|---|---|---|---|---|
| 1a  The role and responsibilities of the senior leader for the school-to-school support in the targeted aspect for improvement is made explicit to the other partner/alliance schools. | | | | |
| 1b  The strategic leader overseeing the school-to-school support work for the agreed improvement aspect has clarified with all partners the aims and purpose of the joint work. | | | | |
| 1c  Challenging and stretching agreed targets have been set between partner schools in the alliance, trust or federation, in relation to the particular school improvement aspect, which indicates high expectations for improvement. | | | | |
| 1d  There is the capacity, capability and commitment from the respective senior and middle leaders in the partner school to drive the improvement forward in the aspect. | | | | |
| 1e  The governing body of each school involved in the school-to-school support work takes an active interest in the ongoing joint activity. | | | | |

*Promoting and Delivering School-to-School Support for Special Educational Needs*, Routledge © Rita Cheminais 2013

## 2 Professional development

| Good practice evidence descriptors | Emergent ✓ (Early stages at 30%) | Developing ✓ (Work in progress at 50%) | Embedded ✓ (Fully in place at 100%) | Evidence and impact |
|---|---|---|---|---|
| 2a Staff involved from the lead school model good practice to those staff in the partner school in relation to the aspect of school improvement. | | | | |
| 2b Coaching is utilised effectively during the school-to-school support and improvement work with relevant staff in the partner school. | | | | |
| 2c Key staff from the lead school mentor other colleagues in the partner school in order to further develop their competency, capability and confidence in the aspect for improvement. | | | | |
| 2d Opportunities are provided throughout the duration of the school-to-school support work, for colleagues from each partner school to observe best practice from SLEs, ASTs or Excellent Teachers in the aspect of improvement. | | | | |
| 2e Regular training and shared professional development opportunities take place within the partner school in the school improvement aspect, to strengthen mutual learning and inform the induction of trainee and newly qualified teachers. | | | | |

## 3 Stakeholder involvement

| Good practice evidence descriptors | Emergent ✓ (Early stages at 30%) | Developing ✓ (Work in progress at 50%) | Embedded ✓ (Fully in place at 100%) | Evidence and impact |
|---|---|---|---|---|
| 3a Key stakeholders (pupils, staff, governors, parents), in both lead and partner schools, are clear about bringing change and improvement in the targeted aspect. | | | | |
| 3b Key stakeholders in each school have been consulted, in order to seek their views about the school improvement aspect of focus. | | | | |
| 3c Working parties, focus groups, including the school council and the family/parent council have been given the opportunity to discuss and share others' views and opinions, in relation to the school improvement aspect. | | | | |
| 3d Other external parties from the local authority, higher education, multi-agency services, voluntary, community organisations to voice their views and suggest ways forward in improving the targeted aspect. | | | | |
| 3e Information has been communicated via newsletters, briefings and multi-media approaches to keep stakeholders in the lead and partner schools informed about the ongoing work in the school improvement aspect. | | | | |

| Good practice evidence descriptors | Emergent ✓ (Early stages at 30%) | Developing ✓ (Work in progress at 50%) | Embedded ✓ (Fully in place at 100%) | Evidence and impact |
|---|---|---|---|---|
| 4a Staff from the lead and partner schools are clear about what collaborative partnership working entails as well as about each other's respective roles, in engaging in the school-to-school support. | | | | |
| 4b Sufficient resources have been made available to enable school-to-school partnership work in the school improvement aspect to be undertaken and sustained. | | | | |
| 4c Sufficient time has been allocated to enable those engaged in the joint collaborative school-to-school partnership working to meet together and discuss any issues, concerns, share ideas and to reflect on practice. | | | | |
| 4d Successful team work is well established between the lead and partner school, in relation to the school improvement aspect, and the contributions of team participants are valued and respected. | | | | |
| 4e Decision-making across the partnership is based on secure evidence gathered from a range of appropriate sources, to inform improvement in the aspect. | | | | |

| Good practice evidence descriptors | Emergent ✓ (Early stages at 30%) | Developing ✓ (Work in progress at 50%) | Embedded ✓ (Fully in place at 100%) | Evidence and impact |
|---|---|---|---|---|
| 5a The lead and partner schools both systematically monitor and review the impact of the school-to-school support work in the improvement aspect. | | | | |
| 5b Quantitative and qualitative data clearly indicates improvement and travel in the right direction in the school improvement aspect. | | | | |
| 5c Relevant key participants and stakeholders from the lead and partner schools feedback their views on the change and improvement outcomes in the school improvement aspect. | | | | |
| 5d The governing body and the senior leadership team in the lead and partner schools receive regular reports and updates on the progress, developments and improvements being made in the school improvement aspect. | | | | |
| 5e The lead and partner school both seek external impartial objective evaluation of the outcomes and impact of the school-to-school support work in the improvement aspect. | | | | |

## 6 Disseminating good practice

| Good practice evidence descriptors | Emergent ✓ (Early stages at 30%) | Developing ✓ (Work in progress at 50%) | Embedded ✓ (Fully in place at 100%) | Evidence and impact |
|---|---|---|---|---|
| 6a Both the lead and partner schools meet to discuss and plan their strategy and campaign for publicising the good practice in the school improvement aspect, within each school, as well as across and beyond the school alliance. | | | | |
| 6b The impact and outcomes from the school-to-school support work are documented and recorded as evidence-based practice via a small-scale action research report, and/ or via cameos/case studies of good practice. | | | | |
| 6c The good practice in the school-to-school improvement aspect is disseminated via the respective school VLE, podcasting, blogs, video conferencing, Live Channel, PowerPoint, to a range of stakeholders. | | | | |
| 6d The lead outstanding teaching school gains local recognition and is held in high regard by parents, the local authority and other interested parties in relation to the aspect of school improvement. | | | | |
| 6e The leader of the outstanding teaching school explores external national recognition for their good practice in the school-to-school improvement work via OFSTED, DfE, through achieving a validated national award in partnership working, or via showcase events such as regional and national conferences, seminars and workshops. | | | | |

 *Promoting and Delivering School-to-School Support for Special Educational Needs*, Routledge © Rita Cheminais 2013

## 2 Producing an action plan

Table 6.3 Action plan for school-to-school improvement partnership working

| Area of school-to-school support | Action/activities | Lead person(s) responsible | Resources | Timescale (from/to) | Monitoring (who, when and how) | Success criteria (impact and outcomes) |
|---|---|---|---|---|---|---|
| 1 Strategic leadership | | | | | | |
| 2 Professional development | | | | | | |
| 3 Stakeholder involvement | | | | | | |
| 4 Partnership working | | | | | | |
| 5 Quality assurance | | | | | | |
| 6 Disseminating good practice | | | | | | |

The outcome from the initial audit will have identified some gaps that need to be developed further and addressed. The headteacher, and the senior member of staff strategically overseeing the award journey from the lead school, need to form a core team, or working group, made up of relevant staff from their own school as well as from the partner school requiring improvement. The tasks to address the gaps arising from the initial audit can then be shared out to members of this core team. For example, the core team may have the SENCO on it, especially when they are the SLE supporting the other school requiring improvement in SEND. The headteacher from the other improving school, along with his or her deputy head or assistant head, will also need to be on the core team.

The members of the core team are responsible for gathering the necessary evidence to build a credible portfolio of evidence, which can be a multi-media portfolio, to reduce the bureaucracy and form a professional development tool. The senior member of staff from the lead school will oversee the progress made towards completing the activities/tasks on the action plan at regular intervals. Ideally, the core team should meet twice a term to undertake the review of ongoing work in the chosen area of school-to-school improvement.

### 3  Building a portfolio of evidence

Building a multi-media portfolio of evidence is essential to demonstrate the effectiveness and impact of school-to-school improvement partnership working that has taken place in the school requiring improvement. Multi-media evidence is encouraged to be collected as this minimises the paperwork, and also results in the production of a professional development tool for sharing best practice with other educational settings.

The electronic multi-media portfolio should have an electronic folder for each of the six aspects on the school-to-school improvement partnership review framework (audit). Each folder should include the relevant evidence to meet each of the five best practice evidence descriptors for each aspect. These must have the number and letter under each piece of evidence in each electronic folder, e.g. 1a, 1b, 1c, 1d, 1e.

Where evidence in one aspect may also be relevant to another of the six aspects on the audit, this can be cross-referenced, rather than including it twice in the portfolio. The evidence may include podcasts, video clips, photographs, signposting to each school's website for documentary evidence and other multi-media evidence. The portfolio should also include the completed audit and the completed action plan. It is advisable to build the portfolio throughout the self-review journey, as evidence may get lost or forgotten if it is left until the end just before the final external validation. The senior member of staff from the lead school should take overall responsibility for compiling the portfolio of evidence. The portfolio contributes to the final validation process, and should be submitted two weeks before the on-site visits take place. This enables the external professional partner to follow up on any evidence in the portfolio, which they may wish to explore in further depth during the on-site visits.

### 4  Final external validation

The final external validation includes the off-site assessment of the multi-media portfolio of evidence and an on-site visit, spent between the lead school and the partner school to see and hear about the impact of the work of the lead school. The professional partner undertaking the external validation may be an outstanding senior leader from another school or academy or PRU.

An example of a final on-site external validation programme is illustrated opposite.

---

***School-to-school improvement partnership on-site external
validation programme***

| | |
|---|---|
| 08.30 | Arrival of the external professional at the lead teaching school |
| 08.40–09.10 | Meeting with the headteacher and senior member of staff overseeing the self-review process and a relevant governor |
| 09.10–09.40 | Meeting with the core team from the teaching school and those involved directly in delivering the school-to-school support |
| 09.45–10.10 | Travel to the partner school requiring improvement |
| 10.30–11.00 | Meeting with the headteacher, relevant senior staff and a governor |
| 11.00–11.30 | Tour of the school with two pupils who have benefited from the school-to-school improvement work that has been taking place |
| 11.30–12.00 | Meeting with relevant staff who have benefited from coaching and mentoring and training delivered by the lead teaching school |
| 12.00–12.30 | Lunch |
| 12.30–13.00 | Observation of lunchtime activities engaging pupils and staff |
| 13.10–13.40 | Snapshot lesson observations of relevant lessons |
| 13.45–14.15 | Meeting with a group of parents of pupils who have benefited from the outcomes of the school-to-school improvement support |
| 14.15–14.50 | Meeting with a representative group of pupils benefiting from the school-to-school improvement partnership working |
| 14.50–15.20 | Travel back to the lead teaching school |
| 15.20–16.00 | Feedback to the headteacher and senior member of staff overseeing the self-review process on the findings from the on-site and off-site external validation. |

Upon achieving a positive outcome from the final external validation, the lead teaching school should share their good practice with other local schools. The partner school requiring improvement should have acknowledged their contribution to some of the collection of evidence.

## Cameo of best practice of SENCO engagement in the self-review quality assurance process

The headteacher of Maple Grange teaching school is participating in the School-to-School Improvement Partnership self-review process, as he is keen to validate the school's outstanding practice in school-to-school support for SEN. His SENCO, Jill, is an SLE in SEN, and she has been working with the senior leadership team and the newly appointed SENCO and SEN governor at Leafy Lane School, which requires improvement in SEN. Jill has established a half-termly meeting with the headteacher and the deputy headteacher and the SEN governor at Leafy Lane School, to review progress in supporting the newly appointed SENCO to set up a whole school SEN system, and lead improvement in SEN policy and provision across the school.

Jill has been coaching the newly appointed SENCO once a week over the last ten weeks at Leafy Lane School. The newly appointed SENCO feels more able to cope with leading change across the school in SEN. He has also observed Jill working in her SENCO role at Maple Grange School. This has enabled the newly appointed SENCO, Peter, to see how Jill supports class teachers in identifying SEN pupils, monitors SEN provision, organises SEN pupil review meetings and evaluates the impact of additional interventions for SEN pupils. Jill and Peter have both kept a learning log, which has recorded all the activities that have taken place, to support Peter in his SENCO role and implement an effective SEN system, whole school. The learning log is a reflective diary, which records the thoughts and feelings of the coach (Jill) and the coachee (Peter). Extracts from the learning log have been submitted as evidence in the final portfolio. A couple of video recordings of Peter engaging in a coaching session delivered by Jill have also been included in the portfolio of evidence. Jill, with the permission of the headteacher at Leafy Lane School, has also produced a series of podcasts, which show Peter and the SEN governor talking about the impact of the support from Jill. Documentary evidence for the portfolio has included SEN pupil attainment data, showing their progress over the last twelve months, survey feedback from staff, SEN pupils and their parents/carers at Leafy Lane School, and minutes from SLT and governing body meetings on SEN.

Jill has played a pivotal role in effecting change in SEN at Leafy Lane School. She has been given the time and support from her own headteacher, who is also a national leader of education. Standards in SEN in her own school have not been compromised, because Jill has an assistant SENCO, who keeps the department operating smoothly in her absence.

Jill was a member of the core team at Maple Grange School. She supported her headteacher in undertaking the initial audit. She identified the staff from both schools who would be best placed to contribute evidence to meet all the six aspects on the self-review framework. Jill viewed her participation in the self-review as a very positive professional development opportunity, and one which externally validated her effectiveness as an SLE, to effect change for SEN in another school requiring improvement.

---

**Points to remember**

- Quality assurance entails the systematic monitoring of all aspects of SEN policy and provision, to check that it leads to improved outcomes for SEN pupils.
- Quality assurance encourages teachers and teaching assistants to reflect on their work with SEN pupils.
- Participating in a self-review for school-to-school improvement support in SEN offers outstanding teaching schools the opportunity to validate their work.
- There are only four stages in the school-to-school improvement partnership quality assurance self-review process: audit, action planning, building a portfolio of evidence and external validation.
- The self-review process is grounded in evidence-based practice.
- The self-review and external validation processes help to disseminate best practice in school-to-school support.

---

## Further activities for reflection

1  As a SENCO, how are you going to quality assure the revised SEN policy and provision in your educational setting?
2  Using the self-review framework (audit) provided with this chapter (Table 6.2), which areas of SEN partnership working with other schools requires further improvement in your educational setting?
3  What would be the benefits to your educational setting in engaging in the self-review quality assurance process, to validate your best practice, in school-to-school support for SEN?
4  How are you evidencing your good practice in school-to-school support for SEN?
5  Which aspects of SEN policy and provision give your educational setting credibility in the local area and why?
6  Referring to the quality assurance indicators for SEN in Table 6.1, which indicator(s) require a greater focus in your own educational setting and how will you address this?

# Glossary

**Academy** is a sponsored or converting school, directly funded by central government, which is independent from local authority control.

**Achievement for All (AfA)** is a whole school improvement programme, which targets improvement in outcomes for pupils who experience barriers to learning, which includes those with SEN.

**Appreciative inquiry** refers to a change management approach that focuses on identifying what is working well, analysing why it is working well and then doing more of it.

**Education, health and care plan (EHCP)** replaces a SEN statement, and sets out the support that a child will need from birth to age twenty-five. Local authorities and health services are required to work together to plan and commission the required support. The plan gives parents the same statutory protection as a SEN statement.

**Evaluation** is the systematic process of collecting evidence to make an objective assessment about the effectiveness and impact of an initiative or change. It also helps to identify strengths and weaknesses, and inform decision-making, future planning and change.

**Force field analysis** is a useful decision-making technique that identifies and analyses the factors for and against a change, communicating the reasoning behind the decision.

**Free schools** are all-ability, state-funded schools set up in response to parental demand, which are independent from local authority control. They can be set up by a charity, a university, a business, an educational group, by teachers or a group of parents.

**Improving teacher programme (ITP)** is targeted at those teachers who aspire to deliver consistently good lessons.

**Monitoring** is the ongoing process of checking progress against objectives set, which in turn helps to inform evaluation.

**Outstanding teacher programme (OTP)** is aimed at enabling good teachers to become outstanding teachers, who will subsequently assist other teachers to raise their performance.

**Pupil premium** is additional funding targeted at pupils on free school meals, or who are looked after children, or who are children living in an armed service family. The money is used by schools to help close the attainment gap between these vulnerable disadvantaged pupils and their more social and economically advantaged peers.

**Quality assurance (QA)** is the process of systematically monitoring different aspects of a service, policy, initiative or programme, to check that it is 'fit for purpose', meets quality standards and leads to a positive outcome for pupils.

**School self-evaluation** is the process by which a school looks critically at itself in order to improve further the quality of its provision and performance.

**School-to-school support** entails recognising the importance of connections between different issues, individuals and institutions, in order to promote collaboration between schools, with a view to removing educational disadvantage for vulnerable pupils.

**Specialist leader of education (SLE)** is an outstanding middle or senior leader who supports other colleagues in similar positions in other schools to improve.

**Teaching leader** is a middle leader with strong teaching ability and analytical skills, who develops other colleagues professionally in their own school or department, to enable them to improve pupil outcomes.

**Teaching school** is an outstanding school, which identifies and disseminates good practice existing in their own school to their alliance partner schools and to other schools who are in need of improvement.

**Value added (VA)** is a measure that shows the difference a school makes to the educational outcomes of pupils, given their starting point.

**Virtual learning environment (VLE)** is a popular method of e-learning (distance learning), where learning takes place through electronic means using, for example, video conferencing, podcasting, computers and the internet. Pupils are able to access curriculum tasks, resources and online teacher support virtually, via email communication. FROG is an example of a virtual learning platform used by some schools.

# References and further reading

ACAS (2010) *How to Manage Change Booklet*. London: Advisory, Conciliation and Arbitration Service

Audit Commission (2008) *SEN/AEN Value for Money Resource Pack for Schools*. Wetherby: Audit Commission

Cheminais, R. (2010) *Special Educational Needs for Newly Qualified Teachers and Teaching Assistants: A Practical Guide*. London: Routledge

COL (2010) *Quality Assurance Toolkit For Open Schools*. Vancouver: Commonwealth of Learning

DCSF (2009a) *Progression Guidance 2009–2010: Improving Data to Raise Attainment and Maximise the Progress of Learners with Special Educational Needs, Learning Difficulties and Disabilities*. Annesley: Department for Children, Schools and Families

DCSF (2009b) *Lamb Inquiry: Special Educational Needs and Parental Confidence*. Annesley: Department for Children, Schools and Families

DCSF (2009c) *Achievement for All: Guidance for Schools*. Annesley: Department for Children, Schools and Families

DCSF (2010) *Achievement for All*. Annesley: Department for Children, Schools and Families

DfE (2010a) *Progression 2010–2011: Advice on Improving Data to Raise Attainment and Maximise the Progress of Learners with Special Educational Needs*. London: Department for Education

DfE (2010b) *The Importance of Teaching: The Schools White Paper 2010*. Norwich: The Stationery Office

DfE (2011a) *Achievement for All National Evaluation: Research Report DfE-RR123*. Manchester: University of Manchester

DfE (2011b) *Achievement for All National Evaluation: Final Report. Research Report RR176*. London: Department for Education

DfE (2011c) *Support and Aspiration: A New Approach to Special Educational Needs and Disability*. Norwich: The Stationery Office

DfE (2012) *Support and Aspiration: A New Approach to Special Educational Needs and Disability: Progress and Next Steps*. London: Department for Education

Freedman, S. and Horner, S. (2008) *The Report School Funding and Social Justice: A Guide to the Pupil Premium*. London: Policy Exchange

Hargreaves, D.H. (2010) *Creating a Self-improving School System*. Nottingham: National College for Leadership of Schools and Children's Services

Hargreaves, D.H. (2011) *Leading a Self-improving School System*. Nottingham: National College for School Leadership

Hargreaves, D.H. (2012) *A Self-improving School System in International Context*. Nottingham: National College for School Leadership

NCSL (2006) *Network Leadership in Action: Getting Started with Networked School Self-evaluation*. Nottingham: National College for School Leadership

NCSL (2010a) *A National College Guide to Partnerships and Collaborations: Resource*. Nottingham: National College for Leadership of Schools and Children's Services

NCSL (2010b) *Schools Leading Schools 11: The Growing Impact of National Leaders of Education*. Nottingham: National College Publishing

NCSL (2011a) *Achievement for All: Leadership Matters*. Nottingham: National College for Leadership of Schools and Children's Services

NCSL (2011b) *System Leadership: Does School-to-School Support Close the Gap?* Nottingham: National College for School Leadership

NCSL (2011c) *Leadership that Promotes the Achievement of Students with Special Educational Needs and Disabilities: Support Pack Resource*. Nottingham: National College for School Leadership

NCSL (2011d) *Specialist Leaders of Education Prospectus*. Nottingham: National College for School Leadership

NCSL (2012a) *Key Facts: Teaching Schools.* Nottingham: National College for School Leadership

NCSL (2012b) *National Teaching School Prospectus.* 3rd edition. Nottingham: National College for School Leadership

OFSTED (2010) *Special Educational Needs and Disability Review: A Statement is not Enough.* Manchester: Office for Standards in Education, Children's Services and Skills

OFSTED (2011) *Special Educational Needs and/or Disabilities in Mainstream Schools: A Briefing Paper for Section 5 Inspectors.* Manchester: Office for Standards in Education, Children's Services and Skills

OFSTED (2012a) *School Inspection Handbook: Handbook for Inspecting Schools in England under Section 5 of the Education Act 2005 (as amended) from September 2012.* Manchester: Office for Standards in Education, Children's Services and Skills

OFSTED (2012b) *Subsidiary Guidance: Supporting the Inspection of Maintained Schools and Academies from September 2012.* Manchester: Office for Standards in Education, Children's Services and Skills

OFSTED (2012c) *Inspecting the Effectiveness of Partnerships: Briefing for Section 5 Inspection.* Manchester: Office for Standards in Education, Children's Services and Skills

OFSTED (2012d) *Additional Provision to Manage Behaviour and the Use of Exclusion: Briefing Paper for Section 5 Inspection.* Manchester: Office for Standards in Education, Children's Services and Skills

Teaching Leaders (2011) *Teaching Leaders, Participant Experience,* http://www.teachingleaders.org.uk/participant-experience,17.html, accessed 15 June 2012

The Sutton Trust Education Endowment Foundation (2012) *The Teaching and Learning Toolkit.* London: Education Endowment Foundation – The Sutton Trust

The Sutton Trust (2011) *Toolkit of Strategies to Improve Learning – Summary for Schools Spending the Pupil Premium.* London: The Sutton Trust

# Index

# Pottery

## In easy steps

# Pottery
## In easy steps

## John Dickerson

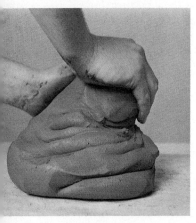
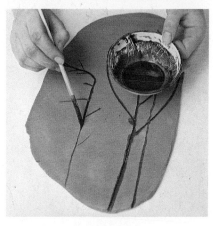

## Studio Vista
## London

Written by John Dickerson
Photographs by Alain Le Garsmeur

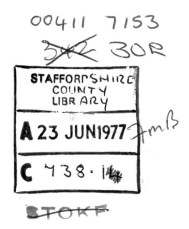

A Studio Vista book published by
Cassell & Collier Macmillan Publishers Ltd.,
35 Red Lion Square, London WC1R 4SG
and at Sydney, Auckland, Toronto, Johannesburg,
an affiliate of
Macmillan Publishing Co. Inc.
New York.

ISBN 0 289 70721 8

Set in Times Roman By RSB Photosetting, Lightwater, Surrey, England.

Printed in The Netherlands by Smeets Offset, Weert

# Contents

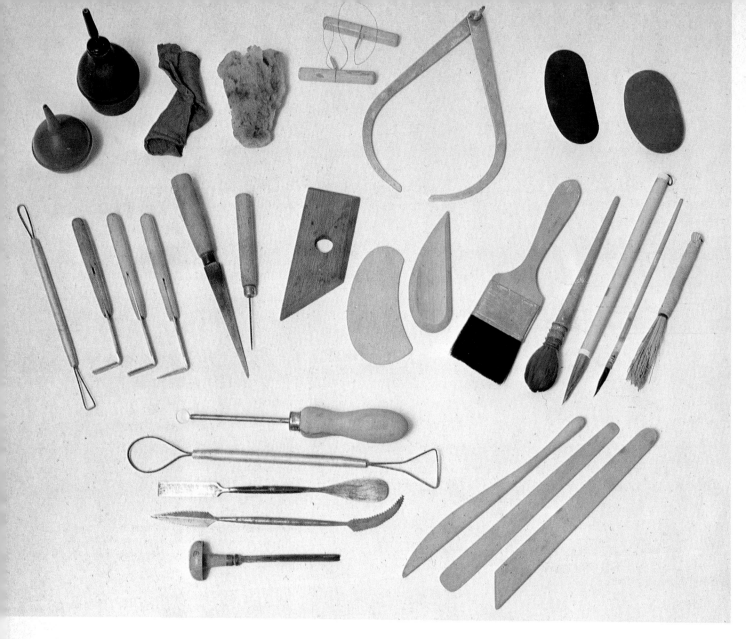

6

# Introduction to pottery

All the general purpose tools and equipment you will need to make the projects in this book. Numbers in brackets refer to pages where they are introduced and you can find out more about them. From left to right (top row): *Slip trailers* (42). *Chamois leather* and *'elephant ear' sponge* – needed for throwing (24). *Potter's wire. Calipers* – for measuring thrown forms (31). *Steel and rubber palettes or scrapers*. (Middle row) *Clay turning tools* – you will need a selection of profiles. *Potter's knife* and *potter's pin* – essential equipment. *Wooden ribs* – for throwing. *Brushes* – for decoration (42) and for kiln wash (49). (Bottom row) *Turning, carving and plaster working tools. Fine gouge* – for mishima (46). *Wooden modelling tools* – a selection is useful.

A selection of typical plastic containers and utensils suitable for pottery use. Sieves and a stiff brush, a banding wheel and an accurate weigh scale are among the most commonly used equipment in small studios.

Pottery is perhaps the most appealing of all the crafts and certainly the most widely practised. Since the infancy of our species it has played a fundamental role in providing practical utensils for everyday life, as well as being one of the richest vehicles for the expression of man's artistic impulses.

Two aspects of pottery make it particularly attractive to the beginner. Firstly, you do not have to wait for years to experience a measure of success. Because the processes of pottery are, in essence, such simple ones there is no reason why you should not be pleased with even your first efforts. What is vital is that you should learn carefully the disciplines, possibilities and limitations of each new process. As your projects become more varied or ambitious, you will develop your general understanding of the craft. The second great appeal of pottery is its cheapness. Clay and most other basic ceramic materials are inexpensive to buy and you can, if you wish, supplement these with materials you glean from nature. Tools and equipment also need not be expensive: most potters prefer homemade or simple tools and the studio equipment you require depends upon the project you plan to tackle.

Many people like to begin pottery by joining a class or club where a variety of materials and equipment are available. In this way you can experiment and find which are most suited to your needs and preferences before you buy.

This book offers you a series of projects which allow you to learn most of the basic processes of pottery. It shows you how to decorate and glaze your work and also how to prepare, pack and fire the most common types of electric kiln with safety and efficiency. But, perhaps more importantly, it demonstrates that working with pottery is enjoyable, satisfying and exciting and lays sound foundations in the craft that will allow you to move on to more advanced and ambitious work.

# Clay Preparation

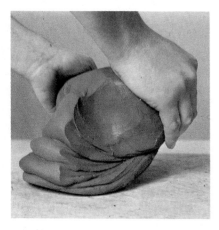

**1** Working on a firm surface, press with the heels of both hands into the rear of the mass.

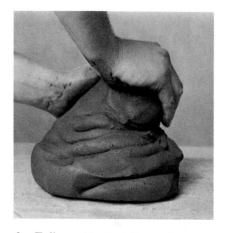

**2** Follow with a twisting and compressing action in which pressure from one hand predominates.

**3** Spread grog on the work surface. Knead the clay on it until all has been absorbed.

**You will need:**
Plaster slab
Potter's wire
Grog
Damp cloth or plastic sheeting

The basic material from which all pottery objects are made is clay. Clays are earth minerals which have been derived by the processes of weathering and hydrothermal degradation of igneous rocks. Millions of years of erosion have reduced the mother rock to extremely fine lamellar particles, which have either been deposited in beds on the site of their formation or have been carried by wind and water to be laid down elsewhere as strata within the earth's crust.

Soil is often erroneously thought of as clay and indeed does contain some clay; but since it is heavily polluted with humus, sand and stones it is useless for pottery. Clay is to be found in the earth in the subsoil stratas and, while it is perfectly possible – even desirable – to dig your own clay from nature, it is normal and much more convenient for the beginner to buy a ready prepared product from a clay supplier. Most suppliers (see page 64) will send you a copy of their catalogue on request. These are well worth obtaining for, besides providing you with information about the individual products which you are interested in buying, they are a source of data and reference material.

Most studio pottery is made from clay which is mixed with just sufficient water to make it malleable. This water, known as pore water, serves the dual purposes of helping to bind the particles together yet at the same time provides lubrication between them so that we have a material which is at one and the same time strong – in the sense that it does not fall apart – and easily modelled and manipulated. The ability of clay to be easily shaped and to retain this shape as it dries is known as 'plasticity' and is the most important characteristic of clay.

The other important characteristic of clay is its reaction to fire. All clays are affected by the application of heat; firstly becoming hard and rocklike but later, if overfired, they soften and eventually melt. The temperature at which a given clay obtains its optimum qualities of strength and resonance is called the maturation temperature.

There are three main categories of clay product:

*Earthenwares* – potteries maturing at 1100°C (2012°F) or less.

*Stonewares* – potteries maturing between 1200–1300°C (2282–2372°F).

*Porcelain* – potteries maturing at above 1300°C (2372°F)

Although several clay types occur in nature only a few are used alone. Normally a number of clays are blended in a carefully designed composition (called a 'clay body') to give optimum working qualities and maturation temperature.

Earthenware clay bodies are those which contain large amounts of easily fusible components, stoneware bodies contain those fluxing agents active at higher temperatures, while porcelain is based on unpolluted china clay and high temperature fluxes. A basic relationship exists, therefore, between the clay with which you work and the temperature to which the piece will eventually be fired.

Pottery suppliers normally sell

**4** Mix two different clays by slicing each mass and interspersing one with the other. Knead.

**5** Cut through with a wire. A marbled pattern clearly indicates an insufficiently kneaded mixture.

clays by weight in one of the following forms.

*A Plastic Clay Body* – a clay blend suitable for a particular firing temperature range, mixed and ready for use. This is the most convenient way to buy, but at least 20% of what you buy is water.

*Dry Clay Powder* – separated and refined individual clays for use by potters who prefer to design and compound clay bodies to suit their individual needs.

*Clay Slip* – a suspension of clay particles in water. Slips are easy to make but you may prefer to buy an industrial product if you are contemplating slip casting on some scale.

Clay for use in pottery then needs to be of the type suitable for the processing intended for it and to be easily malleable without being sticky or unworkably soft. If your clay is too wet spread it out on a wooden board or a slab of plaster of Paris until the excess water has been absorbed. If, on the other hand, the clay is too stiff cut it into thin slices with a potter's wire, moisten each face with a wet sponge and knead the pieces of clay back together into a single mass. Repeat the process if necessary. Finally, the clay needs

to be homogenous, the water content must be uniform throughout the mass and all air bubbles must be removed. This is achieved by kneading.

Although kneading is a two-handed, manipulative process, the real work is done by the weight of the torso and the shoulders, so the surface upon which you work should be at about thigh height. Try to think of your fingers as being joined together: do not let them separate during the kneading process or they will dig into the clay and create pockets to trap air. Do not try to knead too much clay at one time until you have learned the technique.

Some projects recommend the addition of grog (ground fire brick) to your clay (see page 14). Combine this with the clay as part of the kneading process (see **3**).

Test the progress of your kneading by cutting through the clay mass with your potter's wire. No marbled traces of constituents or air bubbles should be evident. Bring the two pieces of clay together again sharply with the full weight of the body behind the action in order to exclude air. Wrap in a damp cloth or plastic sheeting if it is not for immediate use.

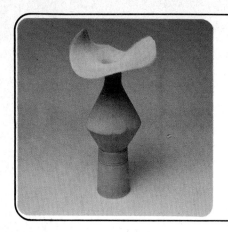

# Pinch Pots

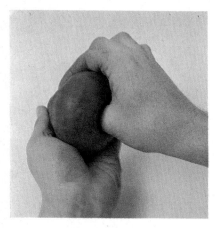

**1** Push the right thumb into the centre of the clay. Thin walls by pinching between thumb and fingers.

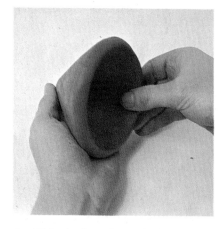

**2** Thin the form from the base upwards. Consolidate the lip; moisten it slightly if cracks appear.

**3** Use a potter's pin to score the lips of each component. Apply coats of thick slip to each.

**4** Press the modules together so that slip is exuded. Use your finger or a tool to weld the joins.

**You will need:**
Fine, plastic clay
Potter's pin
Slip
Brush
Wooden paddle
Scrapers

Pinching small pots from balls of clay, using only the fingers as tools, is one of the most ancient of pottery techniques. Although it can be thought of as being the simplest pottery forming technique it is capable of exhibiting refined and subtle qualities.

The clay for making pinch pots should be fine in texture and of good plasticity. It must not dry out too quickly from contact with the hands and must not be prone to cracking or tearing. A plastic earthenware body containing about 15% of the finest grog is ideal. It should be in a very malleable condition without being sticky and must be well kneaded.

The bowl is the normal product of the pinching process. Cylindrical shapes can be made, but conical ones are preferred. More complex forms, such as the bottle shown here, are made by joining two or more basic bowl modules.

Correct action by the two hands

during the pinching process is the key to success. The left hand has two simultaneous functions to perform. Firstly, the whole hand has to be held in such a way that it both cradles and supports the shape of the developing form. Secondly, it has to turn the form constantly so that it may be thinned and modelled as it passes through the right hand. The right hand is used exclusively for thinning and shaping the walls. Keep the fingers together and thin the walls with a gentle squeezing action between them and the thumb.

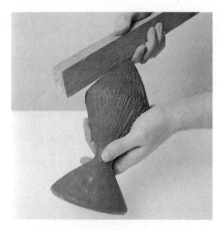

**5** Use a piece of wood to beat the pot gently into shape before cutting open the neck orifice.

An optimum thickness of wall for pinch pots is 5mm ($\frac{1}{4}$in.) or less. Model the whole of the bowl within the supporting cradle of the left hand (see **2**).

Cracks in the walls are usually the result of poor technique, but this can also be caused by the clay drying out too quickly. In this latter case cover the pot with a damp cloth for a few minutes, smooth over the cracks with the fingers and continue pinching.

Model the lip of the bowl with care; damp it lightly if it has a tendency to crack and strengthen it by compressing it gently with the index finger while supporting the walls with the thumb and second finger.

When finished, bowls should be stood on their base so as not to mar the lip. Pieces that are to be components in bottle forms may be stood on their lips to stiffen.

In order to make the bottle illustrated, model up three basic bowl forms. The first two will be joined lip to lip to form the belly of the pot (so they need to be of the same diameter). The third will be joined foot to foot with the inverted second element and re-pinched *in situ* to form the wide flaring lip.

Pinch up all three bowl forms on the same occasion and from the same batch of clay. Allow the first two to stiffen in the air for a few hours but keep the third slightly softer by covering it loosely with plastic sheeting.

Mix some of the clay body with a little water until it is reduced to a slip the consistency of thick cream – this is used an adhesive in joining the clay modules. Leave the pot to stiffen overnight before cutting the neck aperture through into the belly of the pot.

When the basic forming of the pots is complete keep it uncovered in the damp cupboard for a few days, as a result of which it will have stiffened to a largely inflexible condition (termed 'leather-hard'). The surface of the pot can now be finally refined by being cut, pared down and scraped. Surform tools, hacksaw blades and scrapers made from pieces of flexible metal are all suitable for this task. Finally, if you wish, you can burnish all or part of the surface of the pot with the back of a spoon.

Handle the pot with increasing care as it dries, since it becomes extremely brittle after the leather-hard condition.

**6** Support the upper component carefully as you refine its shape into a decorative form.

**7** When the whole pot has stiffened scrape down its surface to reveal the final form.

# Coiled Pots

**You will need:**
Plastic clay
Wooden board or bat
Knife or potter's pin
Wooden paddle
Surform tools
Scraper

The technique of building up pieces of pottery from coils of clay is very ancient. It does not require such precisely disciplined manipulation as the pinch pot (page 10) but it is vigorous and direct and it allows us to build up very large forms comparatively quickly and easily. Coil building may be used to make pots of any shape, but its most common application is to produce large, asymmetric forms. (Symmetrical forms are much more easily produced by other methods.)

Clay for coil building may be of any of the common body types, provided that it is reasonably plastic. Generally it should include 10-15% mixed fine and medium grades of grog (although for very large pots, such as this, increase this amount by a few percent and include larger grades of grog). Make the clay up to a fairly soft consistency, since rolling the coils tends to dry it considerably.

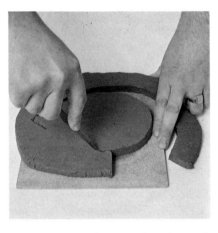

**1** Cut a base of appropriate size and shape from a slab of clay approximately 19 mm ($\frac{3}{4}$ in.) thick.

Knead the clay thoroughly before you start work.

It is best to build your pot on a bat (see page 25) or wooden board so that it can be turned and moved as necessary. If you have access to a bench banding wheel (see page 6) use this to carry the bat or board.

It is desirable to have a fairly well evolved visualization of the shape you plan to make before you begin.

Start by making the base of the pot (see **1**, page 14). Then make up a whole batch of coils at one time before going on to use them. The coils should be about 25mm

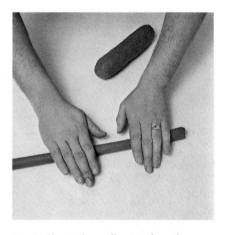

**2** Roll out the coils. Apply only moderate pressure and use the full areas of the hands.

(1in.) thick and completely round. Wrap them in plastic sheeting as they are made to keep them damp and malleable until they are needed.

Begin making the pot by scoring the perimeter of the top surface of the base with a potter's pin or the tip of a knife. Apply a coat of thick slip and place the first coil on this prepared area, pressing it down well. Cut off any excess coil and join the two cut ends together carefully to form a complete ring.

Secure the first coil to the base within the pot by pushing down a little of the clay from the coil and

**3** Use a finger to press down a little clay from the coil and weld it securely to the base.

**4** Stagger the joins in subsequent coils. After adding several coils weld together on interior.

**5** Weld coils together in the same way on the exterior before continuing to build the pit.

welding it into the clay forming the base.

The second coil is joined to the top of the first and the two welded together on the interior surface. It is not essential to apply slip between coils although some potters prefer to do so. Do not allow joins in coils to be located vertically above one another as this creates a line of weakness within the wall of the pot. If the form of the pot is intended to belly out as it rises add each coil slightly towards the outer edge of its predecessor. In convergent forms coils are added a little towards the inner edge of the one beneath.

After about eight coils have been added, weld over the joins and adjust or consolidate the shape if necessary, paddling the walls with a piece of wood (**6**). When making large pots, particularly when they are divergent in shape, it is best to allow them to stiffen in the air over night at this stage to prevent the form from slumping. Before setting it aside, however, it is advisable to wrap a strip of damp cloth around the top coil and to cover this with a strip of plastic sheeting. When you resume work on the piece, score the lip with a potter's pin and

**6** As the form progresses use a wooden paddle to beat the clay walls into the desired profile.

**7** Refine the surface of the completed pot with surform tools and finally scrapers.

apply slip before you add further coils.

The forming procedure then continues until the full height of the pot is achieved, at which point in time the whole piece should be encased in plastic sheeting and left in the damp cupboard (see page 48) for a minimum of 24 hours so that moisture can equalize throughout the piece and thus reduce drying strains.

You can then undertake the final shaping of the piece by further paddling. Use shaped paddles to obtain special profiles. Do not try to alter the form too radically or too quickly and allow the clay to settle between short sessions of paddling.

Should you wish to have a neck or high relief surface decoration on your pot this should be coiled or added onto the form after the general shape has been achieved, followed by another session in the damp cupboard.

The final refinement of the surface of the pot is not undertaken until the whole piece is of leather-hard consistency, when it may be planed, cut, scraped or textured as required.

13

# Slab Pots

## You will need:
Clay and grog
Large piece of cloth or sacking
2 spacing sticks
Large rolling pin
Knife or potter's pin
Slip
Scraper

The construction of pots and ceramic sculptures from flat slabs of clay is one of the most popular of the hand building processes.

There are two main problems encountered in making slab pots: the joins between the slabs tend to split open and the flat sides of the form tend to warp and distort. Insufficient care taken when making the joins and strains set up by uncontrolled drying account for the first of these. The second is the result of poor technique or due to an unsuitable clay body.

## Grog
The material made from crushed fire brick and known to potters as 'grog' is one of the most useful components that can be included in a clay body.

There are a number of valuable characteristics which grog imparts. It opens up compact clay bodies and promotes trouble-free,

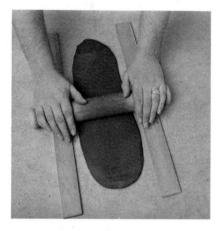

**1** Turn the clay frequently during rolling. Use spacing sticks to achieve desired thickness.

**2** Draw the shapes of each component part onto stiff card and use these as templates for cutting the clay.

**3** Score the site of each join and apply coats of thick slip before luting the slabs together.

**4** Weld the slabs firmly together. Join a thin coil of clay into each interior corner of the pot.

The slab-building technique can be applied to the production of a variety of flat faced forms.

easy and rapid drying. Because grog is pre-fired it reduces the overall shrinkage during drying and firing. It also facilitates successful joining of clay components and minimizes warping.

Up to 30% grog may be added to a body for slab building, but it is suggested that you start with about 20% for this first project, composed of equal amounts of fine, medium and coarse grades.

Begin with a fairly plastic red clay or mix some red earthenware clay into a stoneware body to give it some colour. Combine the grog with the clay as described on page 8.

This table garden is a deep, sheer-sided tray made from five slabs of clay raised on a simple rectangular foot made from four more clay strips. The five slabs should be made in a single session to minimize differences in consistency and moisture content.

When the basic form has been made wrap the whole construction, on its board, in plastic sheeting (see page 48) and leave it in the damp cupboard for at least 24 hours to allow moisture to equalize throughout the piece. After this period remove the plastic sheeting and allow the piece to stiffen in the damp cupboard till it has achieved a leather-hard condition. Return the piece to the damp cupboard after the foot has been added.

You need only glaze the inside of the piece so it is waterproof. The natural, rock-like surface of the unglazed exterior will look right as it is.

Colour can be added through the use of colour slips or a wash or light spray of metallic oxide mixed in water (see page 37).

**5** When the pot is leather-hard lute on the slabs which form the foot. Score and apply slip to all joins.

**6** When the whole pot has stiffened uniformly scrape down the exterior walls and corners.

15

# Moulded Dishes and Pots

**1** Draw the shape of the mould on a piece of board. Use scrap clay to make an inverted model of the form.

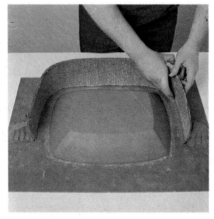

**2** Construct a strong retaining wall around the model. Seal all joins with clay.

**3** To make plaster, sieve dry plaster and sprinkle evenly over water till no free water remains.

**4** Mix by hand to disperse lumps. Allow to stand until first signs of stiffening then pour immediately.

**You will need:**
Piece of board
Scrap clay and plastic clay with
  grog
Sieve
Bucket
Plaster of Paris
Newspaper
Strip of linoleum
String
Scrapers and surform tools
Rolling pin and spacing sticks
Sponge
Potter's wire
Rubber scraper
Plastic sheeting
Potter's pin
Slip

Plaster of Paris moulds are much used, both in studio and industrial pottery, for the production of moulded or cast clay forms.

The press mould detailed here will allow you to make moulded dishes, moulded pots and relief or free-standing sculptures.

The mould is made by covering a clay model of the form required with plaster of Paris. The model can be regular or asymmetric in shape, but keep it fairly simple for your first effort. Size, again, is a matter for your personal choice, but a maximum

**5** Pour plaster over the highest point of the model so that it flows down to cover all its modulations.

**6** When the plaster has set remove wall. Scrape down any irregularities on exterior of mould.

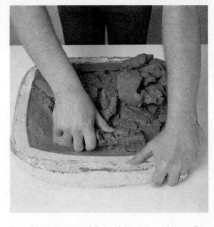

**7** Invert mould and remove board. Release the clay model. Scrape down imperfections in the cast.

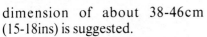

dimension of about 38-46cm (15-18ins) is suggested.

Do not under any circumstances wash the remains of the plaster down the sink.

Put aside the clay used in mould making for future use. Never return clay polluted with fragments of plaster to your general clay stock.

Now that we have one or more press moulds, we are able to consider some of their possible applications to pottery.

## PRESSED DISHES

The most basic application of the press mould is in producing dishes.

Pressed dishes are made from rolled out slabs of clay and any plastic clay body which contains 10-30% of grog will be suitable. (Use a fine grade of grog if you want a smooth surface on the dish.

Roll out the clay (see page 14) until it is several inches larger than the mould in all dimensions. Lower the clay into the mould and trim off the surplus.

Polish the interior surface of the dish and refine the shape of the lip with a damp sponge and a rubber kidney.

Leave the dish in the mould to

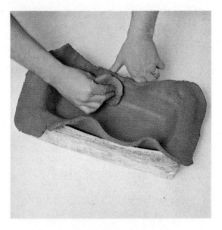

**8** Roll out clay slab. Lower it carefully into the mould. Use a moist sponge to press into recesses.

**9** Trim off surplus clay which projects above the face of the mould. Refine the lip.

**10** Remove the semi-stiff dish from the mould by inverting it onto a board. Enclose in plastic sheet.

**11** Score both lips with a potter's pin. Apply several applications of thick slip to scored areas.

17

**12** Leave one dish in the mould. Join on the other lip-to-lip. Use a tool to weld the two forms together.

**13** Weld slabs onto prepared areas of the pot to form a foot. Paddle them into line with the pot walls.

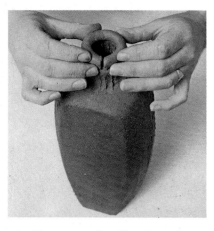

**14** Pierce a neck orifice through into the pot and coil up a suitable neck form around it.

**15** When the whole piece has become leather-hard refine the surface by planing or scraping.

stiffen overnight and remove it the next day.

Scrape or plane the exterior of the form, should it be necessary, with the dish in an inverted position. It may be turned right way up when it is leather-hard in order to refine the lip or to add decoration to the interior, but it should be turned back onto its lip, preferably on a slatted shelf, to dry. In this way severe warping is usually avoided.

---

Glazes which suggest the action of natural process offset the geometry of this moulded bottle.

## CERAMIC MURALS OR WALL SCULPTURES

Attractive relief wall murals or wall sculptures can be made from basic modules formed in press moulds. While the clay is still fairly soft and supported by the mould, penetrations can be cut through the walls of the dish, shapes removed or pared back, parts of the dish wall bent to change the basic profile and decorative walls, partitions, bridges or projections cut from additional clay slabs can be luted onto the interior surface of the form (see page 40).

A number of these units may be laced together, attached to a panel with epoxy resin cement or cemented into a wall to form a large scale sculptural relief panel.

## MOULDED POTS

Large, unusual and exciting pots can be produced from a single press mould. Two moulded dishes are joined lip to lip, paddled into shape and completed by the addition of a neck and foot.

Final shaping of the piece is effected by planing and scraping.

Finally, the neck opening can be cut and a suitable tool inserted to weld over the main interior join between the two dishes.

## FREE-STANDING SCULPTURES

Constructions of this type are made in the same manner as the moulded pots just described, except that a number of press moulds are employed to yield moulded slabs having a variety of profiles and curvatures. It is, of course, not necessary to use the moulded dish shapes whole. They can be cut into suitable components before or after being removed from the mould and used as you please in a wide variety of combinations.

# Slip Cast Forms

**1** Pour casting slip into the centre of the mould until it stands up slightly above the face of the plaster.

**2** When a suitable deposit of slip has been found on the walls of the mould pour out surplus.

**3** Allow the mould to drain by resting it, inverted, on two boards over a bowl or bucket.

**4** Fettle (trim) off unwanted deposits of slip from the face of the mould with a steel palette.

**You will need:**
Casting slip
Plaster mould
Bowl
2 boards
Scraper
Plaster
Fine abrasive paper

A further application of plaster moulds in pot making is in the slip casting technique. Slip is a fluid consisting of a suspension of clay particles in water. In the casting technique plaster moulds are filled with a carefully prepared slip and allowed to stand full for a short length of time. During this period the plaster absorbs water from the slip and a layer of clay is deposited on the walls of the mould. The surplus slip may then be poured off and the cast within the mould allowed to stiffen and later removed.

Casting has the advantages of allowing quick and easy repetition of forms and also allows pots of extreme thinness, delicacy and precision of surface to be made.

**The mould**
Do not be too ambitious over the scale of your first slip-cast piece. Plan to make a reasonably small

19

**5** Pour or splash trajectories of slip onto the surface of a plaster slab to form a lace-like structure.

**6** Separate selected areas of 'lace' from the mass and carefully lift them free from the plaster.

**7** Join 'lace' to the parent form with slip to produce a low relief or free-standing motif.

object and graduate to larger and more complex pieces after you have mastered the process.

You can make up your casting mould from a clay model, as for the dish mould (page 16), or you can attach a piece of leather-hard clay to the head of a potter's wheel (using a little slip as an adhesive) and, using the wheel like a lathe, turn a suitable model with the assitance of trimming tools. A third alternative is to cast part of an attractive natural object, such as half a large green pepper or part of a fruit. The only points to remember in this respect are that since we are making only a one piece mould the cast will not free itself from the mould if it is prevented from doing so by undercutting and, secondly, the model for the mould must either be flexible or of such a material as will allow it to be easily cut out of the plaster.

Use a superfine grade of plaster for your mould and make up your plaster as dense as possible.

'Lace' decoration transforms this slip cast pot from a simple, easily reproduced utensil to a unique object.

### The slip

Casting slips are unlike an ordinary mixture of clay and water in two respects. Firstly, they are largely non-plastic and shrink little. Secondly, the water content of a casting slip is converted into a charged electrolyte by the addition of small amounts of substances termed deflocculants. This causes the charged clay particles to repel one another rather than stick together. The result is that a fluid slip can be made using a great deal less water than is usually the case, giving the benefit of less shrinkage, cracking and distortion.

Buy a ready prepared earthenware casting slip, mix it before use and pass it through a fine sieve to remove any lumps.

### Casting

Make certain that the mould is clean and fairly dry. Paradoxically, if it has been allowed to dry out completely wipe over its interior surface with a clean, moist sponge.

If it is a new mould, never previously used, a 'waste filling' is recommended to remove plaster scum. Prior to filling the mould for the first cast, pour the slip slowly from one jug into another, allowing it to flow gently down its inside surface, and repeat until no further air bubbles are seen.

Use a wide-necked jug to fill the mould. Pour in the slip evenly and not too quickly. Do not allow it to run down the sides of the mould and do not stop or hesitate in your pouring until the mould is full. Fill the mould so that a slight protuberance of slip can be seen above the face of the plaster. As the plaster begins to absorb the water the level of slip will fall. Top up with slip to the original level.

The time it takes for a satisfactory thickness of clay wall to develop depends upon the thickness desired, the absorbency of the mould and the amount of moisture it already contains. Try two minutes for your first attempt and thereafter adjust the time in the light of this experience to produce whatever thickness is required.

When you have achieved the required thickness of clay wall lift the mould carefully and pour the surplus slip out into a bowl (not back into the filling jug if other moulds are to be filled with that mix). Set two boards across the bowl, place the mould mouth downwards upon them and allow the slip to drain for two or three minutes before returning the mould to its normal position.

Trim off the surplus clay that has spilled across the face of the mould as soon as it is stiff.

If you wish to apply free-form 'clay lace' additions to your piece you should begin to prepare them as soon as the main mould has been filled. Wipe over a flat plaster slab with a clean, damp sponge and form your lace by splashing, pouring or trailing casting slip onto its surface. Prepare considerably more than you think you will need. After

Slip-cast lemons shown at various stages of their production. Most fruits can be cast in this way.

about 15 minutes the lace will have dried sufficiently to be lifted from the plaster, trimmed with a sharp knife and bent to shape. Join to the main form with casting slip and press the additions into good contact with the walls of the cast form while it is still moist within the mould.

Twenty to 30 minutes from the time the surplus slip was poured out from the mould is usually a sufficient length of time to leave the cast in the mould. Remove the cast by inversion. (If it is reluctant to leave the mould let it stand for a few more minutes, then jar the mould a few times with blows from the hand.)

You can either rub down imperfections, when the pot is dry or, much less risky, bisque fire it (see page 49) with its imperfections to a low temperature – 750-800°C (1382-1472°F), then rub down with fine abrasive paper.

# Carved Forms

**1** Raise a thick, domed form from a ball of clay by the pinching technique. Set it aside to stiffen.

**2** Cut the exterior base flat and carve a suitable foot-ring from the thick clay that remains.

**3** Carve the exterior walls into the desired form, using knives, surform tools and gouges.

**4** Carve interior of bowl to achieve walls of uniform thickness that relate to exterior profile.

**You will need:**
Clay with grog
Carving and surform tools
Knife or potter's pin
Potter's wire

The Japanese Raku Tea Ceremony bowls are the world's most aristocratic pottery wares produced by the carving process. It is a process which has great potential for creating new and exciting forms, since most of the modelling is carried out upon clay which is already stiff and self supporting. Many of the potter's fundamental disciplines and limitations that derive from the physical nature of soft clay are temporarily set aside to reveal a stimulating range of new skills and formal structures.

A good carving clay can easily be produced from any standard earthenware or stoneware body that has good plasticity simply by the addition of grog. The normal addition is about 35%. For general purposes use equal amounts of fine and medium grades. The inclusion of coarse grog, however, will give a marvellously natural, rock-like quality to the piece.

Carving pre-supposes that you start with a mass of material and that part of this mass is pared away. The clay carver has an advantage over the sculptor in marble, for example, in that his working material is malleable before it stiffens to a condition conducive to carving. During this stage the clay can be beaten and cut to the approximate size and shape of the intended form, thus saving a great deal of work at the carving stage. Carved pots are normally cut from a thick, generalized mass of clay raised to an approximation of the eventual hollow form by rudimentary pinching before being allowed to stiffen ready for carving. The box and bowl here show both techniques of working from a solid mass and from a basic, pinch-modelled form.

The process of actually carving the stiff clay can be done with any cutting tools, such as knives, gouges, planes and plaster working tools.

As can be seen from the photographs, there is a normal sequence of working when producing carved pottery. This involves completing the whole of the exterior form (except, perhaps, for some superficial details) before attempting to refine the interior beyond its most basic shape. It is normal to keep the interior of forms slightly moist with a lightly dampened cloth while the exterior is worked; the interior can then be cut back in relation to the exterior carving to give a uniformity of wall thickness throughout.

Forms should not be allowed to dry out completely until all work on them has been finished, since they become extremely fragile.

Precise control of the form coupled with a rugged and natural appearance are the features of carved wares.

**5** Use a wire to cut an interesting division into a block of fairly firm clay.

**6** Hollow out the basic interior shapes of the two parts to form box and lid.

**7** Carve the exterior into a sculptural form. You will need a variety of carving tools.

**8** Refine the interior of the box so that it relates to your exterior modulations.

# Thrown Cylinder and Bottle

**1** Place clay ball in centre of bat. Beat into cone. With wheel speed fast, lean on clay to centre.

**2** Condition the clay to a circular forming process by pulling it up into an attenuated cone.

**3** Force clay down into a centred disc with pressure from right hand. Control the shape formed with left.

**4** Push left thumb down into centre of disc to leave a base some 12 mm (½ in.) thick.

**5** Push left thumb horizontally across towards left palm to open up the flat interior base of cylinder.

**6** Support pot wall from within. Eliminate any distortion in exterior of disc with gentle upward pressure.

**You will need:**
Moist, well kneaded clay
Small bowl of cold water
'Elephant ear' sponge
Potter's pin
Potter's knife
Potter's wire
Small strip of chamois leather

Throwing on the potter's wheel is the most common of all studio production techniques. It is particularly suited to the formation of symmetrical hollow ware, such as jars, bottles, flower containers, bowls, cups and teapots.

Most potters eventually develop an original throwing technique that suits them, which suggests that there is no one way to throw but many. The technique illustrated here is a good one for those learning to throw since it is relatively impersonal and therefore does not impede the later development of personal solutions. Also, it allows us to separate each stage of the process for individual consideration. Ultimately, of course, all these stages have to be fused together into a fluid process.

Throwing clay must be of good plasticity, moist and well kneaded. Divide your clay into neat balls about the size of an orange.

Potter's wheels come in many different designs. You stand to throw at some; at others you sit. They may be driven by electricity, constant foot treadle action or manual turning. Some have fixed plane metal heads; others are designed to carry 'throwing bats'. These bats are discs, usually of asbestos or plaster, which fix directly onto the wheel head and upon which the throwing is done. You can, if you wish, throw directly on the plane metal wheel heads or, alternatively and preferably, you can attach a plaster bat to them with a little slip.

7  To extrude walls upwards apply pressure to base of exterior. Support from within. Slowly pull hands up.

8  Repeat pull till pot is required height. Smooth rim with a piece of moist chamois leather.

9  Clean up exterior base of wall with a rib or cut in a finger grip with pin and knife. Cut free.

Smear the slip onto the metal head and centre the bat upon it. It will make a firm bond as the plaster absorbs the water from the slip.

Apply a little water to the clay and hands for the purpose of lubrication whenever necessary throughout the throwing process. Brace the arms against the knees or on the side of the wheel basin.

Do not be tempted to miss out on the stage of 'coning up' (2). This is vital to align the constituent lamellar particles of the clay mass.

The bottle form is simply a continuation of the cylinder.

Throw a cylinder of the required diameter and approximate height. Neck in its upper part with gently constricting pressure from both hands (10). As the diameter of the cylinder is reduced the thickness of the clay wall will increase. Ease this clay upwards with an additional pull to form the neck of the bottle.

Necking can also be used to correct flaring in cylinder forms.

Practice is vital for competent throwing. It is probably best not to try to produce pots at the first few sessions but rather to learn the process as thoroughly as possible.

10  Form narrow-necked bottles by constricting cylinder between two hands to reduce diameter. Re-pull.

# Thrown Bowl

**1** To throw bowl, cone and disc as for cylinder, making disc rather wider than for cylinder.

**2** Open up curved interior base of bowl with pressure from fingers working from centre to rim.

**3** Pull up walls to increase size of bowl and flare out to give the required curvature.

**You will need:**
Equipment listed on page 25

The thrown bowl is a seemingly simple form, but such satisfying simplicity is achieved only as a result of considerable aesthetic sensitivity.

The preliminary stages of centering, coning and forming the basic disc from which the pot is fashioned are identical for cylinder and bowl, except that a somewhat wider disc is normally made for bowls.

The first stage of the process is to throw the curved interior base

of the bowl. Since this curve is the key to the whole form of the bowl it must be a carefully considered one. Wet the clay and hands and kick the wheel to a fast speed. With the fingers of the right hand held together, use the left hand to press them down into the centre of the clay before pulling them across in a sweeping, upward curving trajectory towards the right shoulder. As the fingers of the right hand move up and across the disc, allow the thumb of the right hand to move in unison up the exterior wall of the disc to restrain its tendency to flare out-

wards under pressure. The process may need to be repeated several times. Consolidate the lip after each pull.

The width of the bowl is most easily achieved by extruding the walls by the desired amount as a somewhat flaring cylinder, then modifying the curvature with a modelling pull. In this way sagging of the bowl is generally avoided.

Throwing is rather like ballroom dancing in that one partner leads and the other follows. In throwing the bowl the right hand, the initial leader, concedes leadership to the left midway through

**4** Use a potter's pin to cut through the surplus clay at the base of the exterior wall.

**5** Separate this clay from the bat with a horizontal knife cut and remove. Cut pot free with a wire.

the process.

The left hand begins from the centre of the bowl and moves up across the base, getting a sense of its curvature. The right hand applies pressure at the base of the disc and pulls the ridge of clay thereby formed gradually upwards in a near vertical line. When both hands arrive at the wall of the bowl the right one is slightly in the lead and the curving movement of the left forms a curved transition into the wall. The shoulder of the form being passed, the left hand accelerates ahead of the right into the cylinder throwing position and the remainder of the wall is formed in this way as a flaring cylinder.

Once the desired height of the wall has been formed a regular overall curvature of the bowl has to be achieved. This is done with one or two modelling pulls. The assessment and execution of this task lies with the left hand. With the wheel speed medium to slow, the modelling hand begins its work from the centre of the bowl, first assessing the basal curve, then extending it through into the side walls. The right hand supports the clay wall against the pressure from within the bowl and prevents general distortion.

Do not attempt to flare open a shallow bowl in one pull and slow the wheel speed with the increasing shallowness of the curvature.

Once the bowl form is complete remove some of the surplus clay from the base with the pin and knife (as for the cylinder) and cut through the clay with your potter's wire.

Remove the bat from the wheel and allow the bowl to stiffen before attempting to lift it free.

# Trimming
# Thrown Forms

**1** Centre the inverted leather-hard cylinder on the wheel. Use a finger to test centrality.

**2** Attach pot to the wheel with a little plastic clay. Use a trimming tool to refine foot of side wall.

**3** Carefully incise the foot-ring into the centre of the base of pot using a pointed tool.

**4** Cut out the surplus clay from within the foot-ring to produce a recessed base.

**You will need:**
Selection of trimming tools
Small balls of plastic clay
Chamois leather
Chuck (for bottle)

The process of throwing on the potter's wheel produces pots which are thinly and evenly formed, except that in the majority of cases the foot is comparatively thick and unrefined. It can be trimmed to a more suitable profile when the pot has dried to a leather-hard condition.

Trimming or clay turning tools are used for this purpose. They come in a variety of designs and the selection of one type rather than another is largely a matter of availability and personal preference.

**Trimming the cylinder**
Assess the form of the leather-hard cylinder so that you know how much clay to remove and from what areas of the form.

Fix a clean throwing bat on your potter's wheel, invert your cylinder and place it, as nearly as you can, in the centre of the bat. Revolve the wheel slowly, holding a finger (or some other pointer) up against the lowest (i.e., nearest to

**5** Cut away surplus clay surrounding the foot. Continue the line of the walls into the foot form.

**6** Recess base to relate to the curved interior of the bowl. Finish foot with a moist chamois leather.

the bat with the pot in its present position) part of the form that requires trimming. The pot should revolve without gaps appearing between walls and marker. When the cylinder is centred secure it to the bat with three small balls of plastic clay. Use your trimming tool as illustrated to refine the base areas of the pot in the following stages.

Trim the unrefined exterior part of the pot.

Flatten the foot with a number of slow horizontal cuts.

Mark the position of the intended foot-ring with a pointed tool.

Recess the area contained within the foot-ring. This should be flat, relating to the flat interior of the cylinder. The clay left should be about the same thickness as the walls of the pot.

Shape the profile of the foot – a slightly rounded profile gives the pot more stability.

Smooth the surface of the foot-ring with a damp piece of chamois leather.

### Trimming the bowl

The basic processes involved in trimming the cylinder are also applicable to the bowl, except that you must protect the bowl's lip. A number of methods are used to facilitate this. Some potters throw up a dome of plastic clay on the wheel to support the inverted bowl; others cover the face of the wheel or bat with a thin, flat slab of plastic clay. The bowl can be centred on this slab and held with three small balls of plastic clay.

Follow the steps described above for the cylinder. Take particular care, however, to make the shape of the foot grow naturally out of the form of the bowl. The area within the foot-ring should be curved both to follow the general line which runs through the bowl and to relate the exterior to the interior of the form.

### Trimming the bottle

Trimming the bottle presents no new or special problems, except that the neck is too narrow and too fragile to support the pot in an inverted position. You need to use a chuck, which consists of a collar of clay attached to the wheel head in which the bottle is stood. Chucks may be thrown up from plastic clay when needed, or an alternative and more common method is to make a number of chucks of various shapes and sizes, bisque fire them (see page 49) and keep them for use when the need arises.

Soak the chuck in water and centre and attach it to the wheel bat exactly as if it were a pot to be trimmed. To protect the surface of the bottle and to provide a grip, line the mouth of the chuck with a thin strip of plastic clay.

Trim as previously described, remembering to relate the exterior form to the interior profile.

**7** Trim the bottle within a prefired clay chuck. Line mouth with clay to grip and cushion pot.

**8** Once the bottle is centred in the chuck trim the base by the standard technique for cylinder forms.

# Composite Thrown Forms

**You will need:**
Equipment listed on page 25
Slip

A large variety of forms can be made by combining two or more thrown parts. In this project a simple conjunction of bowl and cylinder forms are used, in typical fashion, to produce a compote dish or goblets.

Most of the skills required for this project will have been learned during earlier ones but, since the key to a successful production of these forms is precision of working and foresight, it is useful as a means of developing your skills.

Bowl and cylinder forms are thrown separately and allowed to stiffen somewhat; the bowl is then trimmed to a suitable profile and the cylinder immediately attached to the inverted bowl while it is still in the trimming position. The cylinder is then re-thrown or modelled as necessary to produce a harmonious relationship with the bowl.

Since the centre of gravity is high in forms of this type, the design of the foot area is important if the piece is to have stability.

Use any standard throwing clay body for this project. Remember that the surface of the goblets will come into contact with the lips when the pot is in use and a clay which gives a pleasant smoothness of surface is to be preferred.

Throw the bowl element in the normal manner, as described on page 27. Since it will not need a foot-ring, it is not necessary to leave as much clay as usual at the base of the form.

The cylinder element may be thrown as it will be used or inverted, whichever is more practical for the design of form being attempted.

**1** Throw up the two component parts: a bowl form and a stem (a variation on the cylinder).

**2** Trim the bowl element to have a rounded base and an even thickness of wall throughout.

**3** Score the base of the bowl where it is to receive the stem and the seat of the stem itself. Apply slip.

**4** Use a tool or finger-tip to ensure the two elements are securely welded at point of contact.

**5** Throw any necessary modifications into the stem. Smooth with a moist chamois leather or fingers.

Allow both elements to stiffen in the damp cupboard (see page 48). In this respect some forethought must be given to the amount of modelling which still needs to be done to the cylinder. If it has been thrown to what is virtually its final form both bowl and cylinder elements may be allowed to dry equally until in a soft leather state (do, however, cover the neck of the cylinder element with a small piece of damp cloth). If the cylinder still requires considerable modification cover it loosely with a piece of plastic sheeting so that it remains slightly more malleable than the bowl.

Trim the bowl to a domed base as shown. Measure the diameter of the cylinder neck and score the base of the bowl to receive it. Apply a liberal coating of slip to both contact surfaces before joining one to the other. Before you make too permanent a joint allow the wheel to revolve slowly and check that the cylinder is vertical. With the wheel revolving slowly, throw over the weld on the exterior and use a tool to weld over the join within the cylinder.

Re-throw or model the cylinder as necessary and cut off any excess at the foot with your potter's pin. Finally, smooth the foot of the form with a piece of moist chamois leather.

Return the composite piece to the damp cupboard for at least 24 hours to allow moisture to equalize. (If the cylinder element was much damper than the bowl at the time of joining wrap the piece in plastic sheeting for 24 hours and then allow another day at least in the damp cupboard.)

# Hanging Planter

**You will need:**
Equipment listed on page 25
Cord

The planter consists of two parts, made in the same way.

Wedge 15% fine grog into a good plastic throwing body. Centre up a fairly large mass and, as for a bowl, form a rounded interior base, leaving a considerable thickness of clay beneath it.

Pull up the walls to form a convergent bowl form. If the clay is soft by this time let it sit in the open studio for an hour before flaring over the top 50mm (2in.) to form the rim. Allow to stiffen in the damp cupboard (see page 48) until leather-hard.

Using trimming tools, cut back the thick clay to produce a sculptural motif for the base of the pot and a pleasantly shaped lower form to the bowl. Drill down the centre to form a drainage hole.

Allow the moisture content of the piece to equalize in the damp cupboard, then cut 3 or 4 holes in the rim. Let dry slowly. The supporting cords pass through the central hole in the top, so make it large; rub down all sharp edges.

Fire the form to its maximum strength. No glaze is necessary.

**1** Throw a large bowl form. Make walls rather higher than usual. Flare out rim and turn it over.

**2** Trim away the thick clay from the base of the bowl to create a decorative motif.

**3** Make the base relate well in visual terms to the bowl. Pierce a drainage hole into bowl.

**4** Cut four holes through the rim to accept supporting cords. Make lid in same manner.

# Jug and Teapot

**1** Support the wall of the pot on either side of the point where the lip is to be pulled.

**2** Use a stroking motion with fingers to pull the pouring lip. Smooth rim with a chamois leather.

**You will need:**
Equipment listed on page 25
Slip
Calipers

A great many pottery wares are made for use as containers or dispensers of liquid and, while the basic form of jugs or pitchers can be thrown as a variation on the cylinder technique previously described, they usually need lips or spouts added.

**Lips**
The pulled lip is the simplest pouring device to make and requires only a little deft manipulation to the thrown form. Some potters pull the lip directly after throwing; others prefer to pull the lips on a number of pieces after they have had an hour or so in which to lose their first wetness. In any case, it must be done while the clay is soft and very malleable.

Select the point on the rim of the pot where you wish to form the lip and support the adjacent areas of the wall on either side with the index and second fingers of the left hand. The lip is pulled forward between these supports by the right index finger (or two fingers if you require a wide lip).

Remember that the liquid has to flow smoothly from the main belly of the pot, so the lip needs to start from this area. Damp the index finger of the right hand with water and, with a number of firm but gentle upward stroking motions, gradually stretch the clay mouth of the pot into the lip required.

The actual pouring point needs to be quite thin if liquids are not to dribble back down the outside after pouring.

Finally, smooth the lip with a scrap of damp chamois leather.

**Spouts**
Spouts are simply thrown appendages that are joined onto larger forms with a little slip. They are easy to make, but inexperienced potters find difficulty in positioning a spout so that it functions well and still has the appearance of absolute harmony with the larger form.

Throw and trim the body of the pot, but keep it moist in the damp cupboard. Throw a number of small cylinder forms which you consider might be suitable as spouts and allow them to stiffen to a condition similar to that of the pot. Use a potter's knife to shape the base of the spout so that it relates to the area of the pot where it is to be joined.

Pierce the wall of the pot with the perforations that will feed liquid to the spout with a fine hole cutter, a small wood drill or the point of your knife.

Score all surfaces to be involved in the join with the potter's pin, apply a liberal coating of a slip made from the throwing clay in use and press the two parts together.

The spout may be shaped further, and other additions made to the base form, if required, then the pot should be returned to the damp cupboard to allow moisture to equalize.

## Handles

The pulling of handles is an acquired skill and you must not expect instant results.

Start with a thick coil of the same clay as you used to throw the main body of the pot. Make certain it is moist and well kneaded.

Cut off a piece of the coil about 10cm (4in.) long and grasp it in the left hand.

Wet the right hand and extrude the handle between the fingers and the thumb by drawing the hand down the length of the coil. A dozen or more stroking actions may be required to do this. Lubricate the right hand after each pull.

Bend the extruded handles into suitable curves and allow them to stiffen on a board in the open air for an hour or so. Trim off the excess clay and attach the handles to previously scored areas of the pot surface with a little stiff slip.

## Covers

Simple covers are the easiest of all lids to make – just a low trimmed cylinder form which fits inverted over the pot's neck.

Make the cover immediately

**3** Throw a tapered cylinder suitable for a spout. Allow to stiffen before shaping to fit pot.

**4** Score both surfaces with pin and pierce the grid. Apply slip before pressing spout into place.

**5** To throw a cover, measure the exterior diameter of the neck to be fitted with calipers.

**6** This measurement is the internal diameter of the cover which is thrown as a low cylinder.

after the main body of the pot. Use a pair of calipers to measure the exterior diameter of the neck and throw a low cylinder with the same internal diameter.

Allow the pot and cover to stiffen under the same conditions and trim them together.

Attach the cover form to the wheel in the normal manner for trimming cylinders and shape the unrefined base area into the profile required.

There should be an easy fit between pot and cover. If the cover is too tight trim a little clay from the interior wall.

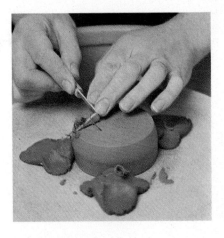

**7** Trim the top of the cover to the desired profile as for cylinder or bowl bases (see page 29).

35

 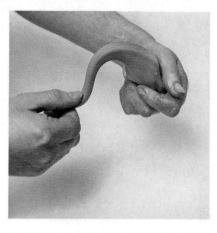 

**8** Pull a handle from well kneaded clay. Grasp clay in the left hand and extrude with the right.

**9** Keeping right hand wet, slowly pull out handle. Bend to shape and leave to stiffen on board.

**10** Score and apply slip to surfaces to be joined. Weld the two parts firmly together.

# Oxides

### You will need:
Various oxides
Scales
Water
Slip
Glaze
Brushes
Organic material
Scraper

The simplest colouring agent in pottery is clay itself, either the natural colour of the clay from which the pot is made or surface dressing of slip derived from a clay which fires to a contrasting colour. In this way a whole range of natural colours consisting of black, browns, earth reds, greys, tans and white are obtained.

Pure clay is normally white and the variety of colours mentioned above result from the fact that the vast majority of clays are polluted by colourants which occur naturally in them in the form of metallic oxides.

The oxides of each metal produce a distinctive colour when used in ceramics although that colour does not always emerge until after glaze firing.

The production or separation of oxides by laboratory or industrial processes have added a wide range of chromatic hues to the potter's repertoire and today, by combining the oxides of various metals together, the potter can achieve virtually any colour he desires.

The word 'oxide' is used as a general term by potters. The material actually used may well be a simple oxide, but it might equally be a carbonate, a dioxide or a pentoxide and still be termed 'oxide'.

Oxides are the most common colourants for glazes and, although some (such as iron and

1   To mix oxides, make a thin, paint-like consistency with oxide, water and slip or glaze.

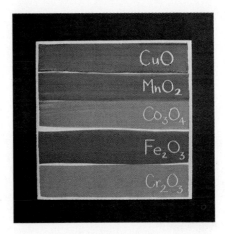

2   The colour effects of oxides in a glaze can be tested by painting onto the surface of a glazed tile.

3   When this tile is re-fired the oxides burn into the glaze and take on their characteristic colours.

manganese) may be used to colour clay or clay slip, ceramic stains derived from oxides are normally preferred for this purpose. Oxides and stains may also be used in a relatively concentrated form as a medium for brushwork and other decorative techniques (see pages 42-45).

The oxides of each metal differ from element to element in their tinting strength and in the percentages that need to be added to a glaze to produce a given strength of colour.

A list of the colours obtained when firing wares in an electric kiln, using the more popular oxides, is given here on the table on the right together with the percentage additions required to produce workable colours.

Single oxides used alone sometimes produce glazes that are garish in colour. Consequently, many potters prefer to mute these colourants with a second oxide. Iron oxide is very commonly used in this way and two typical examples are given below.

Muted green
*Copper carbonate* 3%
*Red iron oxide* 1%

Muted blue
*Cobalt carbonate* 1%
*Red iron oxide* 1%

Nickle oxide ($\frac{1}{2}$-1%) and manganese dioxide (1%) are also popular additions for this purpose and may replace the iron oxide in the above examples and other similar cases.

Black is normally achieved in glazes by using a combination of oxides – a useful one is that given below.

*Red iron oxide* 8%
*Manganese dioxide* 3%
*Cobalt oxide* 1%

| Material | Colour produced | % addition to glaze | % addition to slip |
|---|---|---|---|
| *Tin oxide* | pure white | 5 | – |
| *Nickel oxide* | grey-green | 1-2 | |
| *Iron chromate* | grey | 2 | 2 |
| *Red iron oxide* | red-brown | 4-6 | 3-4 |
| *Red iron oxide* | tan | 2 | 2 |
| *Copper oxide* | green | 2 | |
| *Copper carbonate* | green | 3-4 | |
| *Cobalt oxide* | blue | $\frac{1}{4}$-$\frac{1}{2}$ | |
| *Cobalt carbonate* | blue | $\frac{1}{2}$-$1\frac{1}{2}$ | |
| *Manganese dioxide* | brown | 2-4 | 2 |
| *Manganese carbonate* | plum | 5 | |
| *Depleted uranium oxide* | yellow | 2-7 | |
| *Zirconium oxide (or zirconium silicate)* | hard white | 6-12 | |
| *Chromium oxide* | green | 1-3 | |
| *Rutile (impure titanium)* | cream-tan | 3-5 | |

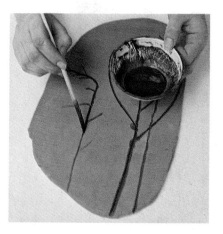

**4** Incised or impressed motifs may be stained with a mixture of oxide and slip for colour contrast.

**5** Remove surplus oxide from surrounding areas by scraping lightly with a steel palette.

Industrially prepared stains are preferred to oxides for the production of certain colours. Stains are particularly popular for colouring clays and slips. Some stains can be used in either clays or glazes but others are suitable for use in only one of these two materials. If in doubt, consult the catalogue of your ceramics supplier for precise details of colours available, applicability and percentage additions.

Stains are the most common glaze colourants in the following cases.

Bright red:
*Cadmium-Selenium stain* 3-5%

Yellow
*Vanadium stain*
*(Tin-vanadium stain)* 4-6%
*or Praeodymium yellow stain* 5%

### Colouring a clay or glaze slip with oxide or stain
First, calculate the weight of the oxide or stain against the dry weight of the clay or glaze you plan to use to make up the slip.

It is very important to calculate the amount of oxide you use precisely. Even so, circumstances affect your results considerably,

and it is as well to remember that a moist clay that does not absorb water gives a thinner result than a more porous one.

Either thoroughly disperse the dry colourant through the dry powder before slaking or, alternatively, mix the oxide or stain with a little water and pass it through a very fine sieve. The sieved material can be added to fluid slip which should first be thoroughly mixed and sieved.

### Making up an oxide mixture for decorating unfired clay
Mix a level teaspoonful of the appropriate oxide (less of the strong oxides of copper and cobalt) with half a cup of water. Add two teaspoons of white slip and mix thoroughly. The resulting fluid is an ideal painting medium for applying brushwork decoration to clay that has dried to a leather-hard condition. See page 42 for some suggestions for decorative ways of applying this mixture.

### Making up an oxide mixture for decorating on top of an unfired glaze film
Mix a level teaspoonful of oxide (less of copper or cobalt oxides)

with half a cup of water. Add two teaspoons of the glaze already used on the piece and mix thoroughly.

Apply the brushwork decoration carefully to the pot as soon after it has been glazed as is practicable.

If you know in advance that you will be applying decoration on top of the glaze surface you will find it advantageous to add a little glaze gum to your glaze slip prior to use. This will strengthen the underlying glaze film and make it more resilient to pressure from the decorating brush.

A transparent glaze softens the line of oxide brushwork when the pot is fired.

6   Natural objects, such as a leaf or grasses, can be used as a mask against background applications of oxide.

7   One of the most common uses of oxides is as glaze colourants.
Percentage additions must be precise.

# Surface Decoration

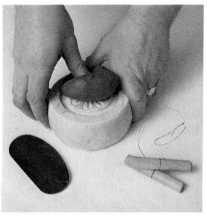

**1** Fill a low relief mould with clay, scrape off the surplus and pull the sprig free when stiff.

**2** Score both surfaces with a potter's pin and apply a coat of slip. Press the sprig into place.

Surface decoration of the raw pot may take several forms, but they fall into the two general categories: articulated surfaces that are the natural result of the forming process and decoration that is added as embellishment to the completed form.

Coil pottery which has not been paddled or scraped down is a good example of the first category.

Combing can also be used in this same manner to impart an overall texture to hand built forms. A random pattern is normally more effective than an attempt to use the comb for regular or fine fluting effects.

A short length of comb can also be used to produce a vigorous, individual incised motif into pottery. This must be executed with verve to be successful. The application of a coat of slip (of a colour which contrasts with the

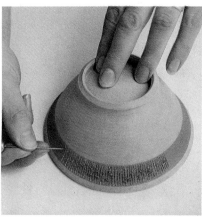

**3** Decorative motifs may be combed into leather-hard clay. Comb through a layer of slip for colour contrast.

**4** Sgraffito is a linear decoration incised into leather-hard clay with a pointed tool.

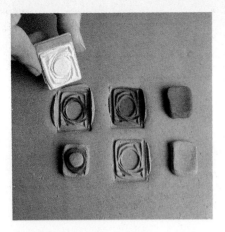

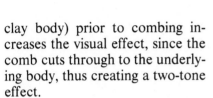

**5** Carved wood or plaster stamps can be effectively used to raise low relief devices on pot walls.

**6** Clay is conducive to being textured in a distinctive way by almost any tool or object.

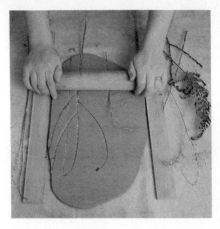

**7** Natural matter can be pressed into clay and left to burn out during firing.

clay body) prior to combing increases the visual effect, since the comb cuts through to the underlying body, thus creating a two-tone effect.

The marks left in pottery surfaces by paddling can in themselves be exciting. Their decorative qualities can be further enhanced by carving decorative motifs into the surface of your paddles. This will be transferred to the clay wall as low relief and can be extremely effective.

Another popular form of surface enrichment can be achieved by beating organic material into the exterior walls of pottery with a paddle. This burns away during the bisque firing to leave a relief impression in the clay. Rice, straw and grasses are the substances most commonly used for this purpose.

Inherent textural decoration may be achieved in slab pottery by rolling out the clay slabs on distinctively textured surfaces such as weathered wooden boards, oriental straw matting or coarse jute sacking rather than the usual, featureless, close-woven canvas or cloth.

Intaglio decorative motifs that are more obviously applied

embellishments may be made by pressing any hard object into the clay surface and removing it to leave an impression. Individual pressings of this type are difficult to make work well but can be effective when used as a frieze running around a form or when a variety of impressions are used together to form a larger, confident motif.

Running frieze patterns (intaglio or low relief) can also be effectively achieved using a simple carved plaster roller. The frieze may be rolled directly into the clay wall or a strip of soft clay may be joined to the wall with slip which, when it is rolled, leaves a raised frieze in its wake.

Relief medallions to be luted or sprigged onto the walls of pots may also be made from cast or carved plaster shapes. The shape is carved, as shown, and the medallion formed by pressing the plaster stamp onto a ball of soft clay. Join the medallion to the leather-hard pot with slip.

Sprig motif (above right) echoes floral shapes. A basic thrown form (right) by Ian Godfrey is embellished with applied motifs.

# Slip Decoration

**1** The colour or surface of clay wares can be changed or modified by a 'dressing' of slip.

**You will need:**
Various slips
Sieve
Brushes
Potter's pin
Banding wheel
Slip trailer
Feather
Wax
Newspaper

Slip is one of the cheapest and most popular decorative materials used in pottery. At its simplest it is a clay or clay body which has been mixed with water and sieved to form an homogenous fluid. Use a

**2** Motifs in slip can be drawn with a slip trailer. Train onto a soft dressing for best results.

coarse sieve to disperse clay lumps when first preparing the slip, but you may well have to use a finer sieve subsequently. Always mix and sieve the slip immediately before use and adjust its consistency to that required by the technique to be employed. (Slip may be thinned simply by blending in additional water. Excess water can be siphoned off from slip after it has settled.)

Always keep your slip in a covered container and do not allow splashes of it to dry on the sides.

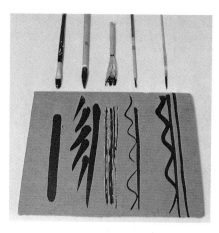

**3** For brushwork decoration select a brush which makes a mark appropriate to the spirit of the design.

## Marbling

Decorating the interior surfaces of moulded dishes with a marbled slip pattern is easy to do and can produce very professional results under a transparent glaze.

Form your dish within the press mould as normal, trim its lip and allow it to stand in the air for an hour or so until its surface has stiffened a little. Prepare and sieve two slips of differing colours. Both should be of moderate thickness so that they retain their autonomy during marbling; on the other hand the slip must be sufficiently fluid to

**4** For marbling, press the interior of the dish with a film of slip and pour off the surplus.

**5** Add contrasting slips and manipulate the dish so that the fluids flow to leave marbled pattern.

**6** Cut or tear pieces of absorbent paper to act as masks and press onto moist clay. Paint over.

flow easily.

Pour the lighter coloured of the two slips into the dish (still supported within the mould) and tilt it so that the slip swills around within the form until all the surface has been dressed. Pour out most of the excess slip which has not been used up in this process by tipping the mould up into a near vertical position (**4**).

Pour some small amounts of the second slip onto the wet dressing. Distribute these additions about the bowl rather than adding all the darker slip in one place. Tilt and roll the mould so that the fluid slips sweep and flow about the form. A marbled pattern of the two colours will gradually develop (**5**).

When you are happy with the effect achieved tip the mould again into the near vertical position and allow the excess slips to run out of the dish. Wipe the edge of the dish with your potter's sponge, allow it to stiffen and remove it from the mould by the normal inversion method when it is leather-hard.

**Cut paper masks**
Cut or torn paper masks may be applied to the surface of a pottery

form, either beneath dressings of slip or between layers of glaze, to produce effects technically similar to wax resist.

Paper mask decoration may be used on any pottery form, but it is most successful on moulded dishes.

Cut or tear suitable paper shapes from any kind of thin absorbent paper (newspaper is ideal) and press them down onto the surface of the moulded dish soon after it is made so that they stick to its surface (**6**).

The bowl may be dressed with a contrasting coloured slip or painted or sprayed over with a thin mixture of slip and metallic oxide. Allow the dressing to become semi-stiff before lifting a corner of each piece of paper mask with your potter's pin. Carefully lift each piece of paper free, bringing its covering of slip with it to reveal the complete two-colour effect (**7** and **8**).

**Painted decoration**
Painted brushwork decoration using slip as a medium is one of the most illustrious of all forms of pottery decoration.

Pointed Japanese calligraphic brushes called *fude* are the best

**7** When the applied slip has stiffened lift the edges of paper with a pin and pull free to leave design.

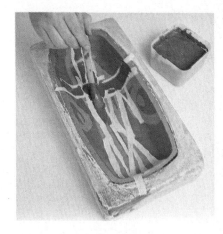

**8** Further masks may be applied and other colours of slip used to create a polychrome design.

43

**9** Some shapes are enhanced by the addition of bands of slip (or oxides) applied on a banding wheel.

**10** For feathered decoration, trail slip onto a fresh dressing of contrasting coloured slip.

**11** Draw a feather or fine brush across the slip trailing to produce the typical pattern.

ones to use, but experiment with a variety of types including some you make yourself from bundles of straw and grasses.

Brushwork can use slip of a colour which contrasts with the clay body colour as its medium or slip coloured with metallic oxides (see page 39) or, indeed, suspensions of metallic oxides in water alone.

It is difficult to give a guide to the best consistency for brushing slip, except to say that it should be reasonably thin and creamy. Test it out on some scrap clay until you arrive at a consistency which suits you. Pass the slip through a fine sieve to disperse any lumps and mix thoroughly prior to use. Apply the slip quickly, surely and confidently.

The oriental slip decoration known as *hakeme* consists of a brief and vigorous application of slip applied with a broad homemade brush of dried grasses. When done well it is impressive under a transparent glaze.

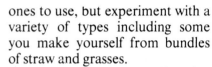

White slip vigorously applied with a homemade grass brush and covered with a transparent glaze (Hakeme).

**12** Paint patterns onto the walls of leather-hard forms with colourless liquefied wax.

**13** Apply slip or oxide. The wax acts as a resist and a two-colour pattern emerges.

## Splashing and whirling

Dramatic decorative effects can be achieved by splashing slip onto a pottery form.

Slip for splashed decoration should be of rather thicker consistency than for brushwork if runs are to be avoided.

Whirling, like splashing, is a dramatic random technique. It is normally used to decorate plates and shallow dishes or bowls.

Attach the leather-hard plate, face uppermost, to your potter's wheel or a heavy banding wheel with some soft clay. (Moulded dishes may be decorated in this way while still contained within the mould). Spin the wheel at a fairly brisk pace and spill some thin slip onto the centre of the revolving plate from a jug or plastic cup. Centrifugal force will throw the slip out towards the circumference to produce a strong decorative device. It is normal to apply two or more coloured slips in this way.

The consistency of slip for whirled decoration needs to be quite thin if a kinetic effect is to be achieved.

## Trailing

The trailing of slip onto pottery wares from a narrow-necked reservoir to produce an active linear design has been popular for centuries.

Slip for trailing needs to be evenly mixed and should be passed through a fine sieve prior to use. It must not be too thin.

The most common form of slip trailer consists of a rubber bulb with a detachable nozzle which allows for easy charging with slip and cleaning.

The slip may be trailed directly onto the semi-stiff clay form but, since this produces decoration with an exaggerated profile, it is preferable to apply a coat of slip (dressing) to the entire surface to be decorated. The decoration is then drawn onto this moist film so that some degree of integration between the two slips is possible (**10**).

A variation on the slip trailing techniques is feathering. Apply alternate trails of different coloured slips to the clay surface and produce the typical pattern by drawing a fine feather across the bands while the slip is still wet (**11**).

## Wax resist

Wax resists and repels water, a fact that allows wax to be used as an effective and simple decorative masking agent against such aqueous solutions as clay slips, glazes and suspensions of metallic oxides in water.

Break up some pieces of white paraffin wax (candle wax), place them in an old saucepan, shallow pan or double boiler and warm over a low heat until just liquefied. Remove the pan from the heat and add thin machine oil – up to about half the volume of wax – and warm the mixture gently, mixing until smooth. The wax solidifies again upon cooling.

The wax may be painted (once a brush has been used for wax keep it for this purpose alone), splashed or dripped onto the surface of any clay form, where it solidifies and thereby masks the application of any aqueous solution (**12**).

Dip the pot into thin slip or paint slip or metallic oxide solution over all or part of the clay form. These materials will adhere to the bare clay, but will be rejected by the wax. The wax burns away in the kiln during firing to leave a two-colour decoration (**13**).

After bisque firing wax resist may be used under or between layers of glaze to produce two-colour glaze effects.

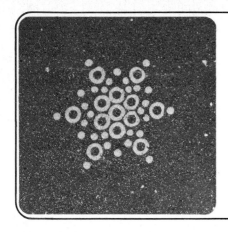

# Inlaid Decoration

**1** Paint the motif onto the form with slip. Cut the pattern into the surface with a fine gouge.

**2** Alternatively, motifs may be impressed into the clay using carved stamps or simple punches.

**3** Pack incisions with stiff slip. Take care to fill the depth of cut. Work along incised lines.

**4** When inlay has stiffened remove surplus with scraper or knife to reveal two-colour motif.

**You will need:**
Stiff slip or plastic clay
Gouges
Cut, carved or cast stamps
Slip and brush (for painting)
Small palette knife
Plastic sheeting
Scrapers

The practice of inlaying materials of contrasting colour into the surfaces of artifacts for decorative effect is common in many of the crafts.

The inlay process as used by the potter is oriental in origin and is properly termed 'mishima'.

Pottery inlay consists of cutting decorative patterns into the surface of leather-hard clay forms or pressing decorative motifs into the clay while it is still semi-plastic. These negative cuts or impressions are then packed with stiff slip or plastic clay of contrasting colour, which is allowed to stiffen. Finally, the excess filling material is scraped off to reveal a clearly defined, coloured motif within the clay surface, which will eventually be allowed to show through a transparent glaze.

Mishima decoration is usually of a linear character, but larger areas can be inlaid if required.

Cutting tools for mishima should be sharp. They should also be of the gouge type, which actually removes a ribbon of clay rather than simply raising a burr on each side of the incision. Linocutting gouges are ideal. Stamps for impressed mishima may be cut from wood, carved from cast plaster blanks or from fine clay and bisque fired before use.

Impress the stamps into the clay when it has stiffened somewhat after forming, but is still less than hard. Support the wall against the pressure from the stamp, otherwise distortions or cracks will develop. Try and push the stamp straight into the clay rather than working it in gradually with a rocking motion.

When cutting motifs into clay walls you need the pot to be in a rigid, leather-hard condition. Some potters like to paint the design they plan to cut onto the pot's surface with slip as a guide before actual cutting begins. You will find that by varying the depth of your cut you can produce varying widths of line.

One of the most common faults is to cut too deeply into the form – about one quarter of the thickness of the wall is the normal maximum.

The filler may be quite simply a plastic clay of a different colour or a coloured slip. White slip may be coloured or the colour of lighter slips reinforced by the inclusion of some body stain or metallic oxide (see page 39). Avoid the more potent oxides such as cobalt and copper, however, since they tend to leave an unsightly blush around the inlaid motif.

A fluid slip may be dried to a stiff consistency by pouring it onto a plaster slab or into a plaster mould for a short time.

Use a flexible metal tool, such as a small palette knife, to pack the filler into the incisions.

Start at one end and work along it rather than trying to fill it all at once or working from both ends. Leave the filler piled up a little above the pot surface.

Wrap the whole pot in plastic for about 24 hours.

Carefully shave, scrape or plane the excess filling material down until the motif appears. It is normally necessary to remove a fine film of the surrounding body before optimum clarity is obtained. The contrast between the two clays will in any case be increased after firing.

The idea suggested earlier (page 41) of pressing grains of rice into the walls of pots is very effective when used in conjunction with mishima. The glaze film builds up in these depressions left after the rice has burned away and provides a subtle new dimension to the decoration.

The use of a transparent glaze accentuates the colour contrast between the clay and the inlay.

# The Damp Cupboard and Drying

**1** Damp cupboard walls must be non-porous. Plaster shelves are ideal: keep then saturated.

**2** You can improvise with a slab of water-saturated plaster, props and plastic sheeting.

**You will need:**
Plastic sheeting
Damp cupboard or box
Strips of damp cloth

Proper drying is vital to the production of pottery wares. Imperfect drying technique is responsible for many of the problems encountered by the hobbyist and student potter.

There are three drying phases which the potter has to control.

**Equalization of moisture**
Whenever additions are luted or otherwise joined onto a pot to form a composite piece the moisture content throughout the whole must be equalized before proceeding to drying. Enclose the whole piece in plastic sheeting for a minimum of 24 hours (longer for larger wares).

**Stiffening**
The next stage is a very slow process of stiffening. This is done inside a damp cupboard or damp box.

The cupboard or box must have a close-fitting door and its interior surface sealed with an impermeable material such as zinc cladding. fibreglass or heavy plastic sheeting.

The atmosphere within must be kept humid, either with a humidifier or with saturated plaster of Paris bats.

Pots will need to be kept in the damp cupboard for about a week.

Thin appendages on pots (such as spouts and handles) tend to dry out faster than the main body of the pot. To prevent fracture wrap these elements with strips of damp cloth.

**Drying**
Once the pots have stiffened they can be brought out into the open air.

Drying shelves should be made of slats of wood or expanded metal so that air can reach all parts of the drying form. Hollow ware is best dried standing on its lip.

Test the ware for dryness against the cheek or inner arm; a cold, clammy feeling indicates the presence of more moisture than in the general atmosphere.

Do not bisque fire wares until they are totally dry. This may take several weeks for thick forms.

Dry, unfired pottery is very fragile and must be handled with great care.

# Packing and Firing the Kiln

**1** Check that kiln shelves are sound. Paint upper surface with bat-wash; clean edges and underside.

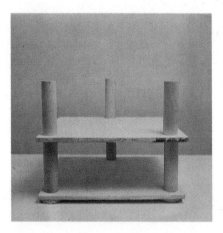

**2** Support each shelf on three refractory props of suitable height. Low ones support effective floor.

**3** Bisque fire pots with lids in place and bowls prone to distortion on their lips.

**You will need:**
Bat wash
Selection of kiln furniture
Pyrometric cones
Pyrometer and thermocouple

### The bisque firing
When pots are completely dry they are ready for the first firing, the bisque (or biscuit) firing. This produces a chemical change in the clay, converting it irreversibly into a hard, rock-like material. Read all the general information on kilns and firing in this chapter before you embark on this process.

Wares may touch one another during this firing so put small forms in larger ones and stack sets of pieces in a lip to lip, foot to foot system, known as 'bungs'. Pots with lids should be fired with the lid in place. Aim for an equal density of pack throughout the kiln.

Fire large bowls standing on their lips and small bowls in bungs to avoid warping. Fire geometric slab pots in the centre of the kiln.

Space kiln shelves evenly and use a three point support system (**2**). Keep pots and kiln shelves away from the electric elements.

If you are using pyrometric cones make certain that you can see them through the kiln peephole when the door is closed.

### Firing schedule
There are a number of possible temperatures for bisque firing, but in the vast majority of cases stonewares and earthenwares can be bisque fired together to about 890-900°C (1634-1652°F).
*Stage 1* – 0–200°C (32–392°F) – The pots contain considerable atmospheric moisture which needs to be dried out very slowly. Leave all the kiln peepholes and vents open and start the firing by leaving

49

the kiln on very low overnight. After 200°C (392°F) all physically held water is released. If this stage is rushed pots made of dense clay bodies will shatter. Beyond 200°C (392°F) the rate of temperature rise may be increased somewhat.

*Stage 2* – 350-700°C (662-1292°F) – Continue to allow temperature to rise at only a modest rate since chemical bonded water is released from the clay molecule now. In fact, most water will have gone by 500°C (932°F), but for chemical reasons it is best not to increase the rate of temperature rise again before 580°C (1044°F). After 500°C (932°F) close any larger vents but leave door peepholes open.

*Stage 3* – Up to 900°C (1652°F) – Organic matter burns out of the clay, carbon is released and inorganic materials convert to an oxidized form.

Allow the kiln to cool slowly and naturally. Do not attempt to open until 200°C (392°F).

Do not handle the wares unnecessarily when unpacking the kiln. It is best to wear gloves.

If the bisque fired wares are not to be glazed for some time, pack them in cardboard boxes or wrap in newspaper.

## THE ELECTRIC KILN

This is normally a heavy gauge metal case lined with refractory fire bricks capable of withstanding high temperatures.

Kilns can be heated by fire from wood, gas or oil but electricity is the most widely used fuel. The interior walls of the electric kiln support coiled kanthal wire elements; some kilns also have elements in the door and floor. Most kilns are front- or top- loading.

Kiln elements can easily be damaged by burning if fragments of clay or glaze fall on them. Use a light brush or a vacuum cleaning

device to remove foreign matter from the kiln before every firing. Handle the elements as little as possible.

## SHELVING

The wares to be fired are stacked in the kiln on shelves; sometimes these shelves are made of refractory clay but more commonly of sillimanite. They are supported on refractory props.

Never fire wares directly on the kiln floor. Raise an effective floor of shelves about 12mm (½in.) above the floor on props. All the props used to carry subsequent shelves must be located vertically above these first ones. Use a three point system with two props at the mouth of the kiln and one prop at the centre back of the shelf. Reverse this pattern for the back shelf of kilns two shelves deep. Do not use cracked shelves (check by tapping) or warped ones.

Shelves are easily damaged by glaze which fuses on them to form glass. Protect them with a layer of bat wash (also called kiln wash) which can be bought from a ceramic supplier or made from 50% kaolin plus 50% flint mixed to a creamy consistency with water. Paint two or three coats on the top surfaces of the shelves only, cleaning up the sides if it runs down. If you are using old shelves chip off any droplets of glaze attached to the bat wash and fill in the dents with more wash. Never invert shelves once they have been coated. Brush down the backs before use.

Kilns fire more evenly if the load is of approximately equal density throughout.

### Temperature

An accurate means of assessing temperatures within the kiln is essential. The first, and best, method is to use pyrometric

**4** Refractory props are available in various designs to suit special needs and personal preferences.

**5** Typical plaques of pyrometric cones showing correct angle of displacement from the vertical.

**6** The cones bend in response to heat allowing you to check firing development.

**7** Pyrometer and thermocouple enable you to assess the temperature inside the kiln with accuracy.

**8** Typical kiln controls include fuses, warning lights and variable energy controller.

**9** Partly unpacked kiln after typical glaze firing showing appearance of wares.

cones, compacted sticks of mixed ceramic materials with a known melting point. You can buy a range of them, covering the full temperature range. Each cone is coded to indicate its temperature equivalent. Cones are placed among the wares in a position where they can be observed through the peephole. By watching for their softening you can see when a given temperature has been reached.

First ascertain the temperature you require – select the appropriate cone with its higher and lower neighbours in the series. (There are international variations in notation systems.) Stand the three cones in sequence in a cone plaque or press them into a small slab of refractory clay (50% fireclay plus 50% grog) at an angle of about 8° from the vertical (see **5**). The centre cone indicates the required temperature. When the kiln approaches maturation temperature you will see the softer cone soften and slowly slump – the rise in kiln temperature should then be slowed. Precise temperatures are indicated at 45° and the required temperature is reached when the middle cone slumps to this angle.

If the third cone slumps overfiring has taken place – information which may be valuable later in diagnosing faults. The kiln may now be switched off or switched over to soak.

The other temperature measuring device is a pyrometer and thermocouple (**7**). The thermocouple is a silica sheath projecting through the kiln wall into the kiln chamber. It contains a bi-metal strip, whose constituent metals have a differing degree of reaction to heat. The pyrometer, which is simply a potentiometer, measures this reaction and translates it into an indication of temperature.

The pyrometer alone is satisfactory for bisque firing but a combination of cones and pyrometer is best for glaze firing.

The controls on electric kilns vary according to model. All are connected to a main power on/off switch – the kiln should never be opened when the switch is on. Most kilns have variable energy controls (0-100% activity) for each electrical phase and a device, most commonly worked through the pyrometer, which causes the kiln to switch off automatically when a pre-set temperature is reached. It is normally also possi-

ble for the maturation temperature simply to be maintained when it is reached; this condition is termed 'soaking' and is advantageous when glaze firing.

Some kilns have sophisticated systems of time clocks which allow the operator to prescribe a complete programme of requirements for implementation during the firing cycle which will then be effected automatically.

In addition, you should have some safety devices on your kiln. It is advisable to have it fitted with a switch which automatically cuts the current flow if the door is opened. The kiln door should also be lockable so that it cannot be opened during a firing. Finally, for the protection of the kiln, a heat fuse which cuts the flow of current should it be inadvertently fired to the limits of its capability is a worthwhile investment.

# Glazes and Glost Firing

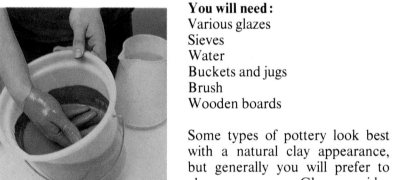

**1** Pass the dry glaze through a sieve to break down lumps prior to slaking.

**2** Mix the sieved, dry glaze with water in a bucket. Disperse all lumps for a smooth, creamy fluid.

**You will need:**
Various glazes
Sieves
Water
Buckets and jugs
Brush
Wooden boards

Some types of pottery look best with a natural clay appearance, but generally you will prefer to glaze your wares. Glaze provides a sealed surface that is non-porous and in which the clay is dressed over with a bonded film of glass-like material which is easy to clean, smooth to the touch and

**3** Brush the slaked glaze through a fine sieve to achieve a completely homogenous fluid.

**4** Test the consistency of the glaze by briefly dipping a bisque fired tile into the slip.

**5** Attach a fired test sample to glaze bucket. Make a note of details and code base of test.

decorative.

Glaze itself may be thought of as a precise mixture of chemicals that, under a controlled application of heat to a given level, form a predetermined type of glass.

It is normally applied to the bisque fired pot as a suspension of the chemical particles in water (called a glaze slip). The ware is sufficiently porous to absorb the water out of this mixture, leaving a deposit of chemicals on the pot's surface.

The first task is to buy or prepare the basic glaze mixture, considering certain factors.

## The maturation temperature
This must be comfortably within the capability of the kiln to be used to fire it. It must also relate to the clay used to form the pot. Earthenware clay pots must be glazed with an earthenware glaze. Pots made with a stoneware clay body will normally be glazed with a stoneware glaze, but the lower temperature earthenware glazes may be used.

Glazes with differing characteristics may be used on a single pot providing that they all have the same maturation temperature.

## Surface
The two most common glaze surfaces are glossy and matt, although there is a range of possibilities between these two extremes. There are also special surfaces suitable for larger pieces and sculpture.

## Transparency
Glazes are normally either transparent or opaque. Transparent glazes are used with decorative effects such as mishima (page 46) and slip painting (page 42), which need to be allowed to show through the glaze. Opaque glazes normally mask the clay surface of

the pot completely.

Some glazes, such as those using borax as a flux, for example, tend to produce a semi-opaque effect.

## Colour
Most glaze bases are, by themselves, colourless or whitish. Any glaze may be coloured by combining appropriate amounts of metallic oxide in the glaze composition. These oxides should be weighed out as a percentage of the total of all the solid glaze components and thoroughly dispersed amongst them before water is added (see page 37).

If you decide to buy a ready prepared glaze you will have little to do other than mix it with water, although you will probably find it advantageous to pass it dry through a sieve first to break down any lumps it may contain.

Alternatively you may decide to compound your own glaze from a recipe. If such should be your intention a brief word of advice here may save you disappointment later.

Glazes are highly variable things. Some components are of uniform chemical composition despite their source; others, particularly naturally occurring components, may differ quite considerably from deposit to deposit. The authors of books you consult probably used their local materials as far as possible and a glaze that worked perfectly for them may require some modification. Some materials may be unobtainable and substitutions will have to be made. Unless you have access to experienced advice, therefore, avoid recipes from books which are imprecise as to details of materials required and recommend foreign products that are difficult to obtain.

Having selected an appropriate

glaze base and gathered together the component materials, decide how much glaze you want to make. 1,000 g (20 lb) is sufficient for a modest batch of wares. Calculate how much of each material you will need and check your mathematics before you start.

Weigh out a precise amount of each chemical, using an accurate beam scale or balance. If any chemical appears to be even marginally lumpy pass it through a sieve and take your required amount from the sieved material.

**6** To glaze small pots, fill with prepared glaze poured from a jug and empty immediately.

**7** Grasp the pot by its foot and push down into glaze so that the exterior is coated. Let surplus drip.

**8** Decoratively shaped areas of glaze can be achieved on exteriors with angled dippings.

**9** Interiors or larger pots can be glazed by swilling with a modest amount of glaze.

**10** Use a funnel to intoruce glaze into the interiors of narrow-necked bottles.

**11** Wax resist can be applied beneath glaze or between two applications of glaze for decorative effects.

**12** The exteriors of pots may be glazed by rotating them in the path of a glaze flow.

**13** Pots that cannot be hand held are normally supported on two sticks and glazed by pouring.

Metallic oxides used for colouring are added to the total batch mass of glaze chemicals. If a glaze requires 10 g ($\frac{1}{3}$ oz) oxide as a colourant for a 1,000 g (20 lb) bath of glaze the composition will be 1,000 g (20 lb) base plus 10 g ($\frac{1}{3}$ oz) oxide. You may well need to use a separate balance suited to weighing very small amounts in order to weigh out the colourants accurately

A thorough and even dispersal of all the materials is essential. Do as much as you can to achieve this condition before slaking the glaze with water.

If no mechanical dry mixing equipment is available pass the combined materials three times through a sieve with a hand mixing between each sieving. If the glaze contains any form of raw lead or other toxic material mix by shaking the chemicals together in a closed container.

To start with you will need about 685 ml (1$\frac{1}{4}$ pints) water for each 810 g (1 lb 12$\frac{1}{2}$ oz) dry glaze. Place the water in a plastic bucket and sprinkle the dry mixed glaze on its surface. Mix thoroughly until a thin, creamy solution is obtained. Test the mixture on a scrap

of fired bisque ware similar to that to be glazed until a brief dipping gives a film about the thickness of thick drawing paper. Mix in additional small amounts of water until this constency is achieved.

It is best to allow the glaze to stand a few hours before use. Mix by hand and brush the glaze through a sieve immediately prior to use.

Scrape down any dry glaze which adheres to the interior surface of the bucket after use into the fluid slip and cover with a lid for storage.

## Glaze application

Glaze can be applied to bisque wares by any of a number of techniques. The pot may be covered by a single glaze or additional applications of the same or other glazes may be made onto this initial film for thicker or decorative effects.

Mix the glaze carefully and thoroughly by hand and brush it through a fine sieve. Test the consistency on a scrap of bisque fired ware prior to use; blend in a little additional water if the slip is too thick.

Wash your hands before you handle the wares to make certain that you do not get grease and dirt onto the surface of the pottery.

The standard technique for glazing small pots can be seen in the illustration. First glaze the interior of the pot by filling it with glaze poured from a jug. Empty the glaze back into the glaze bucket immediately. A film of glaze will be left adhering to the inner surface of the pots which will dry rapidly.

Proceed to glaze the exterior of the piece at once. Grasp the inverted pot by the foot and thrust it down into the glaze so that the slip

A fluid glaze is used here over more stable ones to achieve an active and varied effect.

rises up the sides of the form as far as is necessary. Withdraw the pot from the glaze at once and hold it an angle above the glaze bucket (see **7**) while it drains and dries. The final drip of glaze, which tends to hang from the lip, can be drained off by touching it against the wall of the bucket.

The technique of applying glaze with a brush is little used, except to glaze small areas or apply decorative motifs. Should you attempt to glaze large areas in this manner use a large brush well loaded with glaze and apply it with confident, generous strokes.

A large calligraphy brush can be used to overlay brushwork or splashed glaze onto the overall glaze as soon as it has stiffened.

Dramatic effects can occasionally be achieved with just a single momentous splash of glaze on an otherwise unglazed form.

An alternative method of glazing the exterior of forms that can be hand held is to pour glaze over its surface from a jug. This is a good method of glazing shallow dishes, but it can also be used for bowl and cylinder forms. Use a twisting motion of the wrist to turn the pot into the path of the flowing glaze. This method is particularly satisfactory when you wish the appearance of the glaze application itself to have an intrinsically decorative and organic quality.

Pots which are unusually absorbent are difficult to glaze, since the body dries out the glaze and prevents its flow. Bodies that contain considerable amounts of grog or sand or are highly absorbent should, therefore, be slaked by brief immersion in clean water prior to glazing. Proceed to glaze as soon as the surface is dry.

Forms which are large can have their interiors glazed by pouring in a comparatively small amount of glaze and rotating the piece so that the moving glaze eventually coats all parts of the inner surface.

The exterior of large, heavy or difficult to hold forms is most easily glazed if the pot is stood on wooden slats above a bowl to catch surplus glaze. Stand the bowl on a banding wheel and turn slowly to feed the surface of the pot into the path of the glaze flow.

When glazing narrow-necked forms, such as bottles, use a funnel to direct the glaze into the interior. This prevents an excessive build-up of glaze in the neck areas as well as simplifying the filling of the form.

Wax resist may be applied onto the glaze film as soon as it has dried and the pot re-glazed with a glaze of contrasting colour to produce a two-colour effect.

## GLOST FIRING

### You will need:
Equipment listed on page 49

In most cases the temperature achieved during a glaze firing will be considerably higher than that of the earlier bisque firing.

Brush out or vacuum the kiln, taking particular care to remove all fragments of clay from elements and element housings.

Select the appropriate kiln shelves for the proposed temperature. Check that they are sound and unwarped.

Repair the film of bat wash on shelves, if necessary; clean off sides and brush down reverse of each shelf.

Check that you have enough sound refractory shelf props of suitable dimension.

Set the floor shelves in place on low refractory props (see page 50).

### Preparing the pots
The pots to be fired may now be prepared. Although they may be covered with a wide variety of glazes, they must all have a common temperature. Thus, glaze firings (or 'glost' firings, as they are usually known) are normally referred to as being, for example, 'a cone four firing', which means that all the wares in the kiln have glazes which mature at the kiln condition indicated by the bending of cone four.

Pots for firing should have been allowed to stand between the application of glaze and packing into the kiln so that the water absorbed from the glaze has had a chance to evaporate. However, all pots will contain some moisture.

Clean off any glaze from the foot-ring of the pot which would come into contact with the kiln shelf. If this were not done its melting to a glass during firing and its subsequent cooling would bond the pot solidly to the shelf or, indeed, anything else it touches. Also, since the glaze is fluid at its maturation temperature, it tends to run slightly down the walls of the pot; consequently, it is advisable to clean the glaze from about 2.5 mm (1/10 in.) of the wall above the actual foot.

Pots that have a flat base and no distinct foot as such should have the whole base cleaned of glaze.

Use a moist sponge to clean the glaze from the foot of the pot.

The basic rules to remember in packing glazed wares into an electric kiln prior to firing are:

**1** Pots must not touch one another, although the gaps between them need to be only very small.

**2** Geometric and flat-sided forms, such as slab ports, should be fired near the centre of the kiln to prevent them warping or splitting.

**3** There must be a gap between the pots and kiln elements and between pots, kiln walls and thermocouple.

**4** All shelves must be supported upon refractory props located vertically above those below.

**5** Kiln shelves must not touch the electric elements, or directly face an element if an alternative position is possible.

**6** The density of the kiln pack should be kept as even as possible.

**7** Do not handle the pots unnecessarily.

Sort the pots to be fired into

groups depending upon their height. Alternate the size of the gaps between the shelves to help equalize the density. Choose an appropriate number of refractory props to go with each group. The props should be about 6-12 mm ($\frac{1}{4}$-$\frac{1}{2}$ in.) taller than the height of the highest pot in the group.

Start packing the empty kiln from the back. Place the rear refractory prop(s) in place first, then set any geometric slab pots to be included in this first layer of the pack in place along the centre of the shelf equidistant from the elements. Fill in the remainder of the space, working forwards from the back of the chamber, with whichever pots can be most economically used. Set the front refractory props in position before filling in the space around them.

Lift the next shelf into the kiln and lower it down onto the props, making certain that in so doing you have not tilted one of them out of its vertical position. Check that none of the pots is touching the underside of the shelf. A stepped relationship between the back and front stacks of shelves in deep or large kilns helps to facilitate heat penetration.

Any pots which have glaze close to the base or which have on them a glaze which tends to be more than usually fluid should be raised off the kiln shelf on special kiln furniture (4, page 50).

The plaque of pyrometric cones must be placed within the kiln at a point where the whole plaque may be observed through the kiln's peephole. (In large kilns use a plaque of cones opposite each peephole.) Do not set the cones so that they will come into contact with pots as they bend.

Fill the whole kiln and finally re-check that you can see the cones when the kiln door is closed.

14   Before taking glazed wares to the kiln, check that bases are free of glaze. Wipe off with moist sponge.

15   Set individual pots on refractory props for the glaze firing if the glazes have a tendency to run.

16   Set glazed pots so that they do not touch one another or sides of kiln. Avoid wastage of space.

**Firing cycle**

Lock the kiln door shut and remove bungs from the peepholes in the door. (Some kilns have additional bungs at the top and/ or back and these may also be removed.) Raise the kiln temperature very slowly to 100°C (212°F) and allow the kiln to stand at this temperature for about an hour to drive out atmospheric and absorbed moisture. Temperature may now be raised by as much as 100°C (212°F) in each hour for regular pottery – slower firing is desirable for thick wares or sculptural pieces.

Replace all kiln bungs when 200°C (392°F) has been passed.

Cut back the rate of temperature rise when the kiln is approaching the maturation temperature of the glaze and, in large kilns, adjust the energy regulator controls as necessary to achieve an equalization of temperature throughout the kiln.

During the last few degrees of temperature the rate of increase should be as slow as can be managed. Maintain the maturation temperature for about one hour. This period of soak allows all gases to escape from the glaze and all the resulting blemishes to run smooth.

When the period of soak is completed power may be disconnected and the kiln should be allowed to cool in its completely sealed state. The process of cooling must not be hurried if dunting of the wares is to be avoided. Do not, in any event, attempt to break the seal on the kiln till 200°C (392°F) has been reached and then only open the door about 25 mm (1 in.) at first.

The vast majority of your wares should have fired perfectly, but do not be discouraged by a few faults – it is quite normal.

# The Sawdust Kiln

**1** Lay out the foundation course. This may consist of 8 or 12 bricks depending on capacity required.

**2** Build to full height. Allow slightly larger gaps between bricks in foundation and upper courses.

**3** Pour in sawdust base and load pots in layers with bed of sawdust between each layer.

**You will need:**
7-12 courses of 12 common
    building bricks
Sawdust
Fuel-soaked sacking

The sawdust kiln is one of the simplest and least expensive methods of firing pottery. It produces marvellously rich and varied colour effects and the materials for its use are easily available. Its construction and firing method are so basic that the kiln is well within the capabilities of anyone.

Sawdust kilns are constructed from common building bricks and may be located in any open outdoor space. One of the advantages of sawdust kilns is that very little heat is transmitted to the exterior of the kiln, which means that they can be built and used safely in schools. Sawdust kilns do, in fact, bring pottery and a firing method within the capability of any school, even the most elementary, and any house with a garden.

The average sawdust kiln is constructed from about 90 common building bricks. These are assembled in a loose construction – no mortar, fire cement or any other kind of seal being used between the bricks.

Build the kiln on a piece of flat ground. Lay out the base layer of bricks on the ground, as shown, with the bricks placed on their sides and having their frogs facing inwards. Each wall of an average sized kiln is three and a half bricks in length, giving a total of 12 bricks for each course. Allow a gap of about 6 mm ($\frac{1}{4}$ in.) between each brick unless you are siting the kiln in an extremely sheltered location, when you may find this gap has to be increased somewhat.

The kiln may be between seven and 12 courses of bricks in height, depending upon the number of pots to be fired. Leave 25 mm (1 in.) gaps between the bricks on the top layer.

Fill the bottom 20 cm (8 in.) of the kiln with sawdust, which may be obtained cheaply by the sack from any woodyard. (One large sack of sawdust is usually sufficient for a firing.) Place the first layer of pots, which must be thoroughly dry, mouth upwards, directly upon this mound. Leave at least 50 mm (2 in.) between each pot and the walls of the kiln.

4  Light kiln from the top with fuel-soaked sacking. Get sawdust burning briskly before covering.

5  After firing is completed you will find the fired pots in the ash at the base of the kiln.

This first layer of pots should consist of the largest and heaviest to be fired. All pots included in the firing should be filled with sawdust except for bottles or forms with narrow necks.

Cover the first layer of pots with 5 cm (2 in.) sawdust and add the second layer of wares. Continue in this manner until the topmost tier, consisting of the lightest pots, has been packed. Twelve to 20 pots constitute an average packing. Cover the top layer of pots with 30 cm (12 in.) sawdust. There should be two or more courses of brick above the top surface of the sawdust.

The kiln is lit from the top, using a reasonably large piece of old sacking soaked in paraffin or waste sump oil. Lay the soaked sacking on top of the sawdust and cover most of it with a thin layer, 6-12 mm ($\frac{1}{4}$-$\frac{1}{2}$ in.), of sawdust. Leave the corners of the sacking uncovered and ignite them to start the kiln. As the sawdust on top of the sacking catches fire sprinkle some some additional fuel on top of it until a good intensity of heat is produced across the whole surface.

The kiln may now be covered over with a metal lid, as shown, or with a paving slab or kiln shelf, and in most instances requires no further attention until firing is complete.

The kiln tends to emit some flame between the top layers of bricks for about half an hour, after which smoke is emitted. The amount of smoke released decreases significantly after the first hour. If flames continue after the stated time it is probably due to wind activity and gaps between alternate bricks in the wall facing the wind should be plugged with a mixture of clay and sand or grog.

The sawdust smoulders downwards through the kiln, firing the

pots as it comes to them. You can easily tell how far down the kiln firing has progressed by testing the exterior wall with your hands.

The kiln may take anything between 12 and 36 hours to fire, depending upon the type of sawdust and the atmospheric conditions. A pile of wares will then be found deposited in the bottom of the kiln. These normally feature the varied and attractive effects of contact with direct fire.

For use in schools it is recommended that a second wall with larger – 50 mm (2 in.) – gaps between the bricks be constructed around the whole kiln at a distance of 150 mm (6 in.) from it and that the slab type of cover be used instead of the metal lid, which does become rather hot.

You may increase the temperature achieved within the sawdust kiln somewhat by burning a brisk wood fire between the kiln and this outer wall. Start the fire after the kiln has been lit an hour, burn for an hour and repeat at two-hourly intervals.

Wares to be fired in sawdust kilns should be of an open textured type of clay containing reasonable amounts (20% or more) of grog and/or sand. Although less open wares can be fired in sawdust kilns they are more frequently subject to damage.

Unusually tall wares do not fire well in sawdust kilns and should in any case be packed horizontally.

# Enamels and Beads

**1** Use a palette knife to mix enamel and fat oil to a creamy consistency on a glass slab.

**2** Grind the mixture into a smooth paste by a rotary action with a glass mortar.

**3** Bisque fire pots with lids in place and bowls prone to distortion on their lips.

**You will need:**
Enamels in powder form
Palette knife
Oil
Glass slab
Mortar
White spirit
Clay
Knife
Straw
Emery paper
Slips
Nichrome wire
Glazes

Most pots are considered complete after glazing, but you can still apply further decoration in the form of on-glaze enamels. Ceramic enamel is simply a very low temperature glaze which is painted onto the existing fired glaze surface. Once the enamel has dried the pot has to be given a further firing, which both fuses the enamel to a glass and also bonds it to the underlying glazed surface.

Although enamels can, in theory, be applied to most glazed wares, the base glaze must not be re-melted when firing on the enamels. Enamel decoration is more normally applied onto stoneware and porcelain than onto earthenware, but the process is perfectly applicable to this latter case provided that the subsequent firing is carefully controlled.

Enamel decoration is at its most effective when applied on a plain and featureless base glaze, usually a plain opaque white.

Enamels are usually designed to fuse at 730-800°C (1346-1472°F). They may be coloured with stains or oxides, exactly as glazes are. The most sophisticated enamelled wares are given several firings but it is unlikely that you will want to undertake more than one enamel firing.

**4** Form blanks individually or cut lengths from an extruded coil. Push a straw through centre of each.

**5** Refine the shape of the beads with tools or on a piece of abrasive paper.

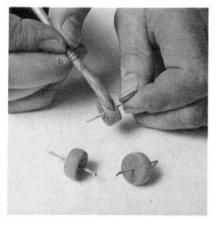

**6** Colour areas of the surface with slips of underglaze colours. Bisque fire when dry.

**7** A simple, slab-built firing frame for beads. Thread them on heat-resistant nichrome wire.

On-glaze enamels (sometimes also called china paints) can be bought prepared and ready for use from most ceramics suppliers. A very wide range of stable, strong colours are available.

Enamels are economical and you need buy only very small amounts. They are compounded into a fluid material by adding either a liquid medium (sold with the enamels) or a glaze gum solution. Mix powder and medium together to get a paint-like consistency. Many potters like to use a glass muller and slab for this mixing process and, indeed, the grinding together of the two materials does seem to improve the workability of the mixture. It should be neither so glutinous that it cannot be applied smoothly nor so fluid that it runs down the form.

Apply the enamel directly with a brush or draw outlines of motifs with a volatile crayon and fill in with enamel. The crayon will burn away during firing.

Fire to the temperature recommended by the manufacturer. Fire the kiln with door peepholes and vents open up to 500°C (932°F). The temperature rise should be very slow up to this point, as the gum has to be burned out of the enamel. Too rapid a rise in temperature will cause the enamel film to peel.

If possible, soak the kiln at the maturation tempetrature of the enamel for about twenty minutes before cooling very slowly.

**Making the beads**
Extremely attractive ceramic beads are easy to make. They are best made with white clay and coloured with oxides, stains and glazes.

Take a well kneaded clay body which contains up to 20% fine grog and roll into thin, even coils; cut with a sharp knife.

Push a piece of dry grass through the centre of each bead and allow to dry. Once dry, remove the grass and refine the shape of the bead with glasspaper or fine files.

Slip decoration may be applied at this stage. Make the slip up to a thin consistency and apply several coats with a brush.

Beads are most easily bisque fired together inside any convenient pot.

Since beads cannot be effectively glaze fired by normal placement in the kiln a special firing frame needs to be constructed, as illustrated. Make the frame by the slab building method from well grogged clay and bisque fire it.

Paint the beads with stains, oxides and glaze in whatever patterns and colours are required. Make certain that the penetrations through the centres of the beads are free of glaze.

Thread the beads onto lengths of nichrome wire and attach to the firing frame, as shown. Make certain that the beads do not touch one another.

The frame may now be loaded in the conventional manner into an appropriate glaze firing.

# Storage and Reconstitution of Clay

**1** Dry, unfired clay may be reconstituted and make workable by simply submerging it in water.

Any pottery studio has two accumulations of clay other than that for immediate use: a general stock of clay and scrap clay. Your general stock needs to be stored carefully, while the second needs to be recycled.

New clay is normally supplied in sealed plastic bags and will remain in good working condition. The clay you are going to use,

**2** When the clay has slaked down, spread it on plaster until stiff enough to knead.

together with similar recycled clay, can be stored in bins of a good size with close-fitting lids.

Cut the clay into fairly large lumps and give it a preliminary kneading. Cover all the clay in the bin with a wet cloth and a piece of plastic sheeting before closing the bin. Keep separate bins for each sort of plastic clay you buy and store grogged clay separately.

Scrap clay is normally fairly plastic, leather-hard or dry. Sprinkle plastic clay with a little water and return it to the stock.

Submerge dry scrap clay in a bin of water, cover and allow to

**3** Store clay in kneaded masses, wrapped in damp cloth, in a lidded container (plastic is ideal).

stand till it has slaked down to the constituency of soft mud. Spread this onto a large slab of plaster or put into large plaster dish moulds. Turn the clay after a few hours. Knead back into working condition the following day.

Alternatively, pound dry clay into small fragments and put them into a plastic container. Sprinkle with water, cover with damp sacking and seal the container. Turn the clay next day and sprinkle on more water. Repeat until the clay has reabsorbed sufficient water.

Leather-hard clay is best reconstituted by drying it out first.

## List of suppliers

*Great Britain*

British Ceramic Service Co. Ltd
Bricesco House
1 Park Avenue
Wolstanton
Staffs

Ferro (GB) Ltd
Wombourne
Wolverhampton

Fulham Pottery
210 Kings Road
London SW6

Pike Brothers
Wareham
Dorset

W. Podmore & Sons Ltd
Caledonia Mills
Shelton
Stoke-on-Trent
Staffs

Potclays Ltd
Wharf House
Copeland Street
Hanley
Stoke-on-Trent
Staffs

*USA*

Alaska Mud Puddle
9034 Hartzell Road
Anchorage
Alaska 99502

American Art Clay Co.
4717 W. 16 Street
Indianapolis
Indiana 46222

Capital Ceramics
2174 S. Main Street
Salt Lake City
Utah 84115

Cedar Heights Clay Co.
Oak Hill
Ohio 45656

Ceramic Colour & Chemical
Manufacturing Co.
Box 297
New Brighton
Pennsylvania 15066

Ceramics-Hawaii Ltd
629 Cooke Street
Honolulu
Hawaii 96813

Dec Ceramics
2401 East 40th Ave
Denver
Colorado 80205

Ferro Corporation
4150 East 56th Street
Cleveland
Ohio 44105

General Refractories Co.
7640 West Chicago Ave
Detroit
Michigan 48204

Hammell & Gillespie Inc.
255 Broadway
New York
N.Y. 10007

O. Hommel Co.
Hope Street
Carnegie
Pennsylvania 15106

Pemco Corporation
5601 Easten Ave
Baltimore
Maryland 21202

Standard Ceramic Supply Co.
Box 4435
Pittsburgh
Pennsylvania 15205

Terra Ceramics
3035 Koapako Street
Honolulu
Hawaii 96819

Van Howe Ceramic Supply Co.
4216 Edith N.E.
Albuquerque
New Mexico 87107

Western Ceramics Supply Co.
1601 Howard Street
San Francisco
California 94103

## Some further reading

*Ceramics – a potter's handbook*
G.C. Nelson, Holt, Reinhard &
Winston, New York, 1964

*Clay and Glazes for the Potter*
Daniel Rhodes, Chilton,
Philadelphia, 1957; Pitman, London, 1958

*An Illustrated Dictionary of Practical Pottery* R. Fournier, Van
Nostrand Reinhold, New York
and London, 1974

*A Manual of Pottery and Ceramics*
David Hamilton, Thames & Hudson, London, 1974; Van Nostrand
Reinhold, New York

*Pottery Making – a complete guide*
John Dickerson, Nelson, London,
1974; Viking, New York

*Technique of Pottery* D.M.
Billington, Batsford, London,
1962; Hearthside, New York

**Acknowledgement**
Pyrometer, thermocouple and kiln
supplied by courtesy of Fulham
Pottery, London (Page 49 and 51).